July 1993

Hope you enjoy unusual sense of humor.

Dick and
Fran
Morris

Get Your Tongue out of My Mouth,

I'm Kissing You Good-bye

Also by Cynthia Heimel:

Sex Tips for Girls

But Enough About You

A Girl's Guide to Chaos

If You Can't Live Without Me, Why Aren't You Dead Yet?

Get Your Tongue out of My Mouth, I'm Kissing You Good-bye

Cynthia Heimel

THE ATLANTIC MONTHLY PRESS
NEW YORK
•

Published simultaneously in Canada
Printed in the United States of America

Library of Congress Cataloging-in-Publication Data

Heimel, Cynthia, 1947–
    Get your tongue out of my mouth, I'm kissing you good-bye / Cynthia Heimel.
    ISBN 0-87113-538-8
    1. American wit and humor. I. Title.
PN6162.H   1993   814'.54—dc20   93-2658

DESIGN BY LAURA HOUGH

The Atlantic Monthly Press
19 Union Square West
New York, NY 10003

FIRST PRINTING

To Gina, Sonny,
and Sugar

Contents

Contents

The Times

Shopping

Battle of the Sexes

L.A.

Contents

i

Foreword
by Brodie Heimel

It was just me and my mom, that's it. When I was a baby, the music of the Rolling Stones (turned up to 11) would never fail to lull me to sleep. I sacrificed peewee league football for art gallery openings and street demonstrations where we'd scream, "Don't buy the grapes! There's blood on the grapes!" My favorite perk, which all of my buddies lacked, was the permission to swear around the house whenever I pleased.

During New York summers, my friends and I would sit on a stoop somewhere in Chelsea. The conversation would eventually lead to the evening's activities.

"What do you want to do?"

"I don't know, what do you want to do?"

"Wanna go over to Brodie's house and say 'fuck' a lot?"

"Yeah."

I got the sense that I was going to be one of those "independent" only children when I was very young. Circa 1974, New York City Welfare

Office. I accompanied my mother on her weekly visits. I call them visits because there was no "pick up the check" at the welfare office. We stood on long lines, anxiously awaiting a fierce battle with a city employee over money for such luxuries as, oh, I don't know, food. Once in a while these funds would contribute to a few cartridges for my Oscar the Grouch Pez dispenser.

"It's so boring here," I complained.

"Then go find something to do. I have to wait here," Mom would reply. Mom was letting me create my own life. I was destined to develop skills in cheese-omelette flipping. I would learn on the street how to fix a game of "Once, twice, three, shoot" so my team could take out the ball first at the cement basketball courts on Ganesvoort. The hardest thing I learned was how to not complain when Mom asked me to run out to get books and juice when she was sick or cheeseburgers and juice when she was writing.

On the welfare line, Mom would say, "Why don't you try the playroom?" after an hour of me drumming on the tile floor.

"They don't have any toys in there." Eventually I would go. There *was* a toy in there. A small truck. It had a broken wheel. All the kids fought over who was going to play mechanic and fix the wheel.

I seem to remember a whole underworld in that playroom. The five-year-old mafia had control of the truck. They would lease out time on it at outrageous prices. The mafia could be bribed with Yankees or Mets baseball cards. Sometimes luck was on my side: the kiddie thug would approach me: "The boss would like to discuss the possibility of your playtime."

That was the birth of my independence. Mom was working her ass off too much to have remaining time for "traditional" family activities. We had our own traditions. My job was to try to complete my mother's thoughts:

"Isn't that the guy from . . ."

"The corner deli?"

"No, that thing with . . ."

"Bigger than a bread box?"

"No, that show . . ."

" 'Hello, Larry'?"

It often took a while.

We would take turns being the Jewish mother. "Look at you dressed that way," I would say. "What do you think all the other kids will think seeing you look like some hippie crazy person?" We'd switch places if I grabbed for the milk while I had a cold: "What are you doing? That's bad for you when you're sick. If you must, don't you drink out of the carton. *I* don't want your germs."

My house was always the house for my friends to go to be teenagers. The two rules were: don't use the Fiestaware as a drum set and whoever was closest to mom at her time of need had to run out and get cigarettes and Diet Pepsi. We were one big happy extended family.

Our front door opened right into my mother's bedroom. I would enter the house followed by a parade of artsy adolescents: "Hi, Mom . . . Hi, Mom . . . Hi, Mom . . ." Sometime later in the evening Mom would open the door to my darkened bedroom. Thirty pairs of young eyes would reflect the hallway light and stare at her like hypnotized deer. "Does anyone want to watch *Annie Hall* with me in the other room?" she'd say.

"No, that's okay, Mom, thanks."

We were happy kids who felt love and support from someone who wasn't afraid to let us be kids. I was probably the most adolescent and the happiest of the bunch.

There's a great deal of history behind these writings. I believe much of my mother's humor developed from her adventures in being the leader of an unconventional family. My mother started as a welfare mother. I had no father around. Yet I was taught to respect others, keep an open mind, and never, ever participate in any riot in a major city. We've been hanging out in Los Angeles lately and the Jewish mother thing is still flipping back and forth: "Don't go in the ocean, you just ate two hours ago."

"You can't dial your car phone from the left lane of the Pacific Coast Highway, you'll *kill* yourself."

Introduction

So how did you like that foreword by my kid? Well written, don't you think? So could somebody out there give him a job? He spends so much time looking, but there's nothing. There's nothing for anyone, which means I should be pleased that, even as I write this, a new administration is setting up shop in Washington. But actually it's been a real pain in the butt.

Couldn't they have waited? Do you know what it's like working on a book while the American presidential elections are going on? Can you imagine how many clever, pungent diatribes against George Bush and Dan Quayle I had to just toss away?

Well, maybe a couple of them slipped in. I couldn't help myself. The goddamned Republican party had been in power for twenty-five goddamned years. (Jimmy Carter was a mere blip in 1976.)

Republicans are kind of like our parents. All their operating principles are based on fear and hatred. Don't go out and play with Jews or blacks or, God forbid, homosexuals. Don't have sex. Don't smoke pot or you'll turn into a crazed junkie.

Above all, don't be weird.

Republicans turned our alleged "land of the free" into a repressive, conformist, judgmental country. They loathed eccentricity. No one was allowed the benefit of the doubt. Even our comedy became the comedy of bullies. Fat and ugly people became the butt of jokes by all bad stand-up comics (who, by the by, are reminding me more than ever of insurance salesmen).

As we have learned from Oprah, repressive parents turn their children into timid, ambivalent creatures riddled with neurotic self-loathing. So it has transpired that the entire population of the United States is a total mess—lacking even a soupçon of self-esteem, unable to commit to anything or have a good time, ever. We are a dysfunctional country in search of a twelve-step program.

But to most of us, the election meant that we've finally overthrown our parents.

Does having a baby boomer in power mean that I have to grow up? Buy a real sofa and matching plates?

And are women really better off now that Anita Hill has spoken up and Murphy's had her baby?

Well, it's nice that we're supposed to be feminists again. That feminism is openly embraced by the media. That nobody bought that "family values" shit for even a minute. That I hardly ever see babes in garter belts on MTV anymore. That a book like *Backlash* was on the best-seller list forever. (I don't want to brag or anything, but I was onto this backlash thing back when it was a gleam in Susan Faludi's eye. I swear. Here's what I wrote in 1988:

It's a plot. Ever since 1970, when feminism took this country by storm, a bunch of think-tank guys have sat around in a room making paper airplanes and trying to wrest all power from women. I know this is true.

"Let's start EST and biofeedback," they said in 1975. "They'll stop thinking collectively and start staring at their navels."

*"Let's get them all to wear business suits and running shoes," they
said in 1980. "They'll start being like smallish men and have coronaries
and die."*

"Now we'll do the biological-clock propaganda," they said in 1985.

*"Okay, let's hit 'em with trumped-up statistics about no men," they
cackled in 1986.*

*"Ha ha, we'll just out and out tell 'em how lonely and miserable they
are," they decided in 1988.*

Pretty good, huh? Okay, so maybe Susan Faludi documented
things just a teensy bit more fully, like 552 pages worth.)

Yeah, things are better. And I personally am proud of us all for
weathering those dark ages. But of course there are still problems.

Like the fact that almost every woman in almost every movie is
still a wife whose big line is "Honey, come to bed." You know the
scenario: The husband is this tortured hero with the weight of the
country or of racism on his shoulders and his wife is always worrying
her pretty little head about how he doesn't spend enough time with the
family. And then near the end of act three they have a big tearful fight
until she finally understands that a man's gotta do what a man's gotta
do.

And there's still no equal pay for equal work. There's still no
decent and affordable child care.

And men and women are still watching each other in utter befud-
dlement. We crave each other more than ever, we've read millions of
books about how to find the perfect mate and what women mean
compared to what men mean and how to fight properly and love
satisfyingly and how not to be afraid of commitment and get what we
need and to stop being in denial and empower ourselves in relationships and we're still just a bunch of morons who have completely lost
the capacity to even say "Hi, what's new?" to anyone we find vaguely
sexy.

No, it's not just you. No one is getting laid. We've examined everything so much, we're so aware of every psychological nuance of every aspect of sexual behavior that all our natural instincts are extinct. Yeats (or was it Blake?) wasn't kidding when he said "Consciousness destroys the act."

I personally have had no choice but to hang around with children. The guys my age are all dating twenty-three-year-olds, and the twenty-seven-year-olds who would normally be dating those twenty-three-year-olds are now going after me. It gets kind of depressing when they've never heard of *Blow Up* or the Bonzo Dog Band.

Speaking of older women, I'm worried about them. There is a chapter in this book about the terrors of becoming a crazy old bat, but it doesn't go far enough. Everywhere I go, I run into perfectly normal, middle-aged women who are flipping out completely.

I blame Budweiser commercials. Specifically this one commercial about a man being reincarnated as a puppy. He's in heaven because he's being kissed and fondled by a gorgeous model. But then the model hands the puppy over to her hideously portrayed grandma, and the puppy wants to kill himself.

What is the point of this misogyny? What the hell is the matter with this society that it feels compelled to ridicule any woman past the age where she is deemed sexually attractive and therefore useful to men? No wonder middle-aged women are going bonkers: First they're zapped by total hormonal chaos that gives them hot flashes and black depressions, and then society tells them that if they're not invisible, they're ridiculous.

When I get older I'm moving to Europe, where old women not only are respected but are encouraged to become as goofy as they want.

"Yeah, yeah," I hear you saying. "If you're such a big feminist, how is it you work for *Playboy* magazine?" This is the second most popular question I was asked during my last book tour, second only to "What was the name of your book again?"

Okay, here's why I work for *Playboy,* and then could everybody shut up about it:

They pay me. They let me write whatever I want except for the time when I combed the Bible to find quotes to prove that Jesus was a homosexual, drug-taking Communist.

("Come on," I said to my editor, "I'm just proving the point that people can find a quote in the Bible to support any hare-brained notion. The radical right is always doing it."

"I don't care," he said. "Do you know the problems we're already having with those right-wing bastards?")

Do you know how many men read *Playboy?* Millions each month, a hell of a semicaptive audience. And the editors at *Playboy* let me attack these men, or even wheedle and whine if I'm so moved. They let me use swear words to my heart's content. They don't even mind if I offend advertisers. Try that at *Vogue.* I did for two years.

Plus I am convinced that if women had auxiliary sex glands in their eyes the way men do there'd be a million women's magazines featuring naked guys right next to the meatloaf recipes. (Everyone knows that only gay men buy *Playgirl.*) Plus, have I mentioned that they pay me?

Okay, the other thing that seems to offend people is that I've sold out and moved from my beloved New York to the dreaded Los Angeles. L.A. is a city with a terrible reputation. They say the people here have no taste, the people here are stupid and amoral.

It's all true. I don't know if I can stand it another second. Not only because it sucks, but I don't think I can ever tune in to this town.

Last month, right before I was leaving to visit New York, one of my dogs ate my best shoes. This was of course a big tragedy, but I had a great pair of shoes in my head and I went out to find them. This always works, because it is a shoe designer's job to be a year ahead of our collective unconscious.

I looked all over L.A. Nothing. Just a bunch of faux Gucci loafers and cowboy boots with rhinestone heels. I grew despondent. I went to New York. I walked down Eighth Street. There were my shoes in every goddamned store.

But can I stand to move back to Manhattan? The homelessness, the winters, the green slime in the gutters? What about my car, my car phone?

What about my dogs? I have four now. My friends tell me if I get any more they'll have to hold an intervention. You'll read about Sally and Doc. But there's also Mike, a little monster who nobody wanted because he's a half inch too big to be a show dog, and Homer, a ten-year-old who was dumped in front of a market where he waited for a week for his owners to come back, the poor bastard.

There are so many great dogs in pathetic situations. Around ten million a year are euthanized in animal shelters. So please, for me, so I don't become the crazy dog lady from whom small children run in terror, spay and neuter your pets.

And listen, if there are any single veterinarians out there who have heard of the Bonzo Dog Band, don't hesitate to write or call.

Feminist

Rants

Boyfriends: Why?

I just want to reiterate something here: *A woman without a man is like a fish without a bicycle.* Old news, you're thinking? An expression that's just too seventies for words? I don't care, I need to trot it out again. I feel too many of us broads have gone astray.

Back in the seventies, in the throes of Women's Liberation, we all smacked our foreheads and exclaimed, "Men: What's the point?" We realized in heady wonderment that while many men are perfectly nice creatures, they are not the point of our existence. We don't need to depend on them financially or emotionally, thank you very much. We don't need them to feel complete. And we certainly, absolutely, no question about it, do not need a man to enhance our status in society.

Then over the years it leaked into our heads that no woman is an island. That although men were not absolutely necessary, life could be a lot more fulfilling with a man in your bed or connecting up your stereo. And this was good.

Then came the dark days when we all fell into the abyss and forgot everything. Then last week we scrambled out of the abyss and into the Year of the Woman.

This much-touted Year of the Woman is a wonderful thing. Consciousnesses have been raised madly. We're ready to deal with sexual harassment and date rape. We've not only discovered but shattered many of those pesky glass ceilings. We've thrown out the dread Pro-Life president and embraced Mr. Pro-Choice. The Senate could now have a women's basketball team if it wanted.

But the personal is political, and I believe that in our personal lives we have forgotten the true status of men.

Too much evidence suggests that too many of us are feeling desperate. Feeling that if we don't have a boyfriend we're ugly and boring and there's something horribly wrong with us. Feeling that we've got to find someone, got to settle down and marry or else we'll be not only miserable but ridiculous.

The pressure is on again, in a big way.

I blame two things: The first is that allegedly scientific but actually pornographic study done in the mid-eighties about the male shortage. You know the one—something about how we had to marry terrorists. The fact that this misbegotten study was disproved didn't matter, every postpubescent female was severely traumatized and immediately stocked up on high heels and lace teddies. You remember. You shudder. Let's drop it.

The second thing is Maggie O'Connell on "Northern Exposure." Yeah, right, it's only a TV show. Only a trend-setting TV show that the thinking members of our culture, the ones who set the pace for the rest of us, look to for role models.

Poor O'Connell. She's in terrible denial. She spends her time looking for love, pretending she isn't. One episode has her falling in love with a man who turns out to be a bear. In another she's convinced that a dog is her ex-boyfriend. Then there was the time she hallucinated all her ex-boyfriends hating her. Lately there's some guy who lives in a bubble but she pines for him anyway. Through it all, she keeps saying, "Come on, I don't need love, I have a career, I'm my own person, I have a career, I'm very happy on my own, I have a career."

And we all snigger because of course she doesn't mean it. The male characters on "Northern Exposure" rarely have relationships, except for a sixty-year-old with a teenager, but they don't mind since they all have adventures. But O'Connell, adventureless, would give up anything for love.

She's so *wistful,* so *yearning* as she's getting kicked in the teeth and ridiculed, just like her forerunner, Melissa on "thirtysomething." I'll never forget an episode of "thirtysomething," I think it was New Year's Eve, where all the couples were cavorting in Hope's house in a soft-focus glow. Cut to Melissa out in the cold, alone, staring forlornly into nothingness.

Let us not forget that the creators of these shows are men, nice men maybe, enlightened men even, but men nonetheless. And men can't help thinking of women only in terms of themselves, as vehicles of sex and romance. Plus all men harbor a dreadful nostalgia for the days when women worshiped them as kings. Who wouldn't?

Let's purge these negative role models from our psyches, let's hearken back to the old days when we had things in perspective. There is no male shortage out there; for people in their twenties and early thirties, there is, in fact, a female shortage. It's the boys who are desperate now, but they're not talking, they're playing it strong and silent, because they figure if they don't say anything maybe we won't notice, maybe we'll run after them, sleep with them, marry them, wash their socks, bear their children, give up our careers.

A woman needs a man like a fish needs a net.

I Wish I Were a Lesbian

A bunch of us went to the theater the other night. We saw a one-woman show starring a performance artist named Carrie, a woman who is funny, moving, attractive, and brilliant. During the show, she talked about being a lesbian, and every time she did, some women in crew cuts and work boots stood up and cheered.

"Those lesbians make me sick," said Carrie later. "I wish they would stop following me around."

"But why?" I asked nervously. With lesbians, I'm always afraid I'll say something politically incorrect.

"They're so damned politically correct," Carrie said. "They reduce me to a stereotype, they're not responding to me but just to my sexual preference, so fuck them." She took another swig of tequila. She was getting very drunk.

My friends were giving a party for her and she loved it. Her eyes were bright, she hugged anyone she could reach. I was fascinated. I'd never met anyone so honest, so warm, so sweet and smart.

Why can't I meet a man like this? I thought as she hugged me. She hugged me again. "You smell so good," she whispered. "Gee, thanks," I whispered back. She kissed me. On the lips. She tried to put her tongue into my mouth.

Oh my God! She tried to put her tongue into my mouth!

I know what guys think, they tell me often enough. They think that if they were women, they would definitely be lesbians. They also think of male homosexuality as a scary perversion, but of female homosexuality as, I don't know, kind of *wholesome.* Hardly anything excites them as much as the idea of two women doing it. (I would like to say for the record that the reverse is not true: The thought of two men doing it turns women off in a New York second.)

"So then what did you do?" asked my friend Brendan.

"I just kept my mouth closed and refused tongue penetration," I said. "I was flattered, but nervous."

"You gotta let her go down on you," he said. "It would be just too cool."

I wish I could.

It was at least a year ago when I had a small epiphany. I was working out at the gym and I saw two women spotting each other while doing bench presses. There was something about them. They seemed so confident, so strong, so self-sufficient. I couldn't understand it. Most women are tentative and conciliatory. They have an underlying urge to please. Most women seem like they're just about to apologize. Not these babes.

They're lesbians! I realized. They don't care if men like them!

I was jealous. I remember only once in my life feeling as content and confident as these women: It was 1979 and I was out of my mind on a combination of Quaaludes and cocaine. This method no longer strikes me as practical.

Oh, to be a lesbian! Never again to become tongue-tied and stupid and self-deprecating and laugh too much! To wear sweatpants my whole life long!

If I could be a lesbian, I could have chocolate cake for dinner every night and still get laid! Men, who have sex glands in their eyes and centerfolds in their hearts, are strange, deranged, picky and exacting about women's bodies! Other women are not! Other women would be empathetic about cellulite and bad-hair days! Plenty of lesbians are fat and loved!

Also, I'd probably drive better. I notice a lot of bad women drivers and I think, If she were a lesbian, she wouldn't be going twenty-five in the passing lane. Because women are taught that to please men, we should be incompetent and fluttery about certain things. We've learned to get hives at the sight of a lug wrench, to faint when a fuse blows. We've been taught that men like us to act as if we can't take care of ourselves. It supposedly makes them feel big and strong.

"I would adore being a lesbian," I told Brendan. "Mentally, I can picture it, but physically, get the fuck out of here."

"Come on, just be bisexual," he said. "Women have such beautiful bodies. Wouldn't you like to fondle a nice breast? Stroke a warm vulva?"

"Now I'm nauseous," I said. I wish I weren't.

What would I say to a lesbian? Men are amazed at how easily women fall into deep conversation the moment they meet. It's because we have a universal icebreaker: men. How annoying they are, how they never listen to us, how we can never figure out what they want, how cute that tall one in the corner is. The subject of men is the leitmotiv of heterosexual women's conversations. When I meet a lesbian, I find myself stopping my sentences in the middle.

But if I were a lesbian, I'd never have to wear one of those newfangled female condoms I've been reading about. Kind of like a diaphragm, only with a tail. A diaphragm with a tail! What fresh hell is this? I read in the paper that the device will "empower" women, that they'll no longer have to "negotiate with a man." Bullshit! The female condom means that women will again be entirely responsible for birth control.

There's that Texas saying, "The trouble with women is they have all the pussy." And the trouble with men is they have all the dicks. (And don't anyone write to tell me that lesbians strap on dildos, because that's the most disgusting thing I've ever heard, if it's even true, which I doubt.)

I am a slave to my hormones. I can put up with a lot of disrespect if a man has nice enough biceps. If he tells me that I should stop being so goddamned successful, that I should wear much shorter skirts and learn how to cook, I whine. I wheedle. I cajole. I try to argue him into having more respect, into being more sensitive—instead of simply telling him to go fuck himself.

If I were a lesbian, I would. Well, maybe. Maybe I'd be just as wimpy with women. Okay, never mind.

Names Are Us

I have this new job: Five days a week, during business hours, I fight about whether women should be called "ladies" or not.

"But why does John have to say 'Hello, ladies,'" I scream at Marco like my life depended on it.

"Look," Marco says, ready to strangle me, "for four years John has called them ladies! That's what he says, goddammit!"

Marco and I work on a sitcom called "Dear John." You know, the one with Judd Hirsch. The guys who work there are getting very tired of the great "ladies" controversy.

I don't care. It's like chalk on a blackboard to me; it's a feminist thing. I thought we had it all settled back in the seventies. Women are not ladies. The term connotes females who are simultaneously put on a pedestal and patronized. A lady is softer and weaker and more dependent than a man. Implicit in the definition is that a man must defer to her, take care of her, because she's not competent to do things on her own.

A lady would never fuck up her nails fixing a carburetor, a lady doesn't swear like a longshoreman during childbirth, a lady doesn't like to give head. At least that's what our mothers told us when we were growing up. They had a whole litany of things that "ladies," which we were supposed to become, were not allowed to do:

"A lady always sits quietly with her hands in her lap."

"A lady keeps her hair nicely combed and out of her eyes."

"A lady keeps her knees together at all times."

I despise this word! Call me a "lady" and I feel like I'm wearing a white dress and can't go splashing through mud puddles.

When women hear a guy say "I want a terrific lady," we know we're dealing with someone with a different frame of reference and we talk slower.

"Okay, then," Marco says every day, "John walks into a room. Three women are standing there. What's he supposed to say? 'Hello, women'?"

There he had me. What's John supposed to say? "Hello, women" sounds really goofy. So would "Hello, men," like you're on a military mission or something. You want something informal, colloquial.

I've searched my brain and discovered something depressing. There is no word in our entire language to define a woman, or a group of women, that is nonjudgmental.

Walk into a room and say "Hello, girls!" and you're either talking to female people under the age of twenty-one or to plumpish middle-aged housewives in fussy dresses who are in the habit of saying to their husbands "The girls are coming over for bridge."

"Gals" means the same thing, except that if the women are grown-ups they're not wearing dresses, they're wearing Bermuda shorts.

"Chick" is another term that diminishes women. It's like "girl" or "gal" only less respectful.

"Babe" implies that a woman is sexually appealing to men, as in

"Is she a babe?" "Well, she's seventy-five-percent babe, but her ankles are fat." Ditto the terms "fox" and (remember?) "tomato."

"Slut" used to mean a slovenly woman. Now it means a woman who will go to bed with everyone. This is considered a bad thing in a woman, although perfectly fabulous in a man.

"Bitch" means a woman who will go to bed with everyone but you.

I want to know why we have no nonjudgmental words to describe us. I want to know why there are no female equivalents to "guys," "fellows," "dudes." I want to know why our language is so goddamned *male,* why everything is defined by how it relates to men.

Why yes, of course there are terms with sexual counterparts. "Spinster" and "bachelor" for example. "Spinster" means you are old and frustrated and unattractive and wear your hair in a bun and have too many cats and probably knit. The worst that can be said of a "bachelor" is he's probably gay.

Then there are those genitalia words. Men can be "dicks," "dickheads," "pricks," "putzes," and I think "schmuck" means penis too. There are so many male-genitalia words because men love penises. All these words mean "kind of a jerk." Whereas there is only one genitalia word for women, "cunt," and it is considered much more obscene than dick et al., because female genitalia is considered much more obscene than male.

Oh wait, I forgot pussy. A word applied to men. It means cowardly, wimpy, weak.

Why are only men "bastards"? Is it that women are considered so insignificant that it doesn't matter if they're born out of wedlock?

Linguists tell us that the language we speak defines the way we think. People whose language includes thirty-two words for snow have a lot more complicated thoughts about snow than we do.

Our language teaches us to think of women as less valuable than men. I hear the word "babe" and I think, "Am I a babe? And if I'm not, am I worthless?" I hear the term spinster and I feel a tiny stirring of fear and distaste before I think, "Thank God I've been married, I'm not a spinster!" I hear "cunt," and before I can stop myself, self-loathing trickles into my soul. I don't want to feel this way. It's unfair for my own language to betray me.

So I have a proposal. Let's make the word "guy" unisex. Let's everybody call each other "guys" so that everybody can feel equal, like they're one of the gang, like they belong. Women do this already, because we utterly refuse to call each other "ladies," but we feel a hint of self-betrayal. If it's made official, we won't.

Okay. We still need a nonjudgmental female word. I think "girl" is sometimes okay, but it's like "nigger": We can use it, you can't.

How about "bitch"? Too negative? I don't think so. A man will call a woman a bitch when he can't control her, when she won't do his bidding, when she's not compliant to his needs. I like this in a word.

Horribly Ever After

Girls! Want to live happily ever after?

Kill yourself now.

Listen, I've been very patient. I've put up with the slow, sure erosion of our dreams, our ideals, our dewy-eyed expectations of a world brimming with child-care centers, with men sharing the dusting, with women going two weeks before remembering to shave their legs.

I hung onto a thread of sanity as hordes of women decided that feminism meant they should turn themselves into small men and wear pin-striped suits and bow ties and pursue the key to the executive washroom as if it were the Holy Grail.

I just hid under the covers when *Women Who Love Too Much* became a best-seller, and women by the scores gobbled the book before breakfast and became convinced that they had this dread *disease* they had to cure before men would want them.

And then the marriage epidemic! And the concomitant baby epidemic! People put blinders on their brains and hypnotized themselves into believing that real life was "Father Knows Best"! And if they couldn't scam themselves into sugar-coated marriages, they blamed it on their codependency problems! So we were back to blaming the victim, but I held my peace. I may have whimpered a little.

But that was then. Now I'm out for blood. No more Missus Nice Girl. Now I've read, in the goddamned *New York Times,* the god-damned Newspaper of Record, that yearning for the handsome prince on the white charger is a perfectly reasonable pastime. That hoping and praying to live Happily Ever After is totally okay. These fantasies, according to the *New York Times,* help us endure.

Endure.

Endure. Jesus motherfucking Christ. Didn't we bury this concept with enormous fanfare in 1972?

I don't blame the writer. I know what it's like to be on deadline. Casting around hysterically for a topic, she realized that all her friends had seen *Pretty Woman* and took it from there.

But because such an idea has been published in the *New York Times,* people will run around believing again that it is true, and they will again start reading *Cinderella* to their four-year-olds. And the whole hideous cycle will be perpetuated.

Believing in the handsome prince on the white charger who will catch you when you swoon and spirit you off to Happily-Ever-After-Land is the utter downfall of women.

Because it is a wish that will never come true. It is a wish that will guarantee that we will never be happy.

It is possible for a woman to be happy with a man, but not if she wants to be rescued. Do you know what kind of guys want to rescue women? Mafia guys! Guys who want to play God! Guys who want total control! These guys are bad news! Tell them you want to take a part-time job and they lock you in a tower!

Plus, if you're waiting around to be rescued you never do any-thing but get your legs waxed. You're too anxious and passive to even read a murder mystery. You've given men all the power, again. You've turned yourself into a giant child.

Girls, what would you do if some adorable guy came up to you and said, "Hi, my life isn't working out at all. Everything's falling apart. Take care of me, please."

You'd say, "Yo, I'm not your mother!" Wouldn't you?

Men are not our mothers. Our mothers are our mothers, and they were the ones who passed on these festering fantasies.

Men are just guys running around who want someone to take care of them too. When we swoon on them, decent men have a tendency to gibber and cry, to feel helpless and inadequate and run away. Of if they're not so decent, they'll lead us on, drop us flat, and steal our wallets.

Wanting to be taken care of is one of your basic human emotions. Our job as humans is to take care of each other. But if we expect rescue as our birthright, if it's supposed to be all one-sided, we're dead. When we don't get it, we're pissed off and crazed, blinded by our own feelings of deprivation, and pretty soon nobody invites us to parties.

Here's my plan: If any girl tells me she rented *Pretty Woman* and suddenly felt a hideous *yearning* bubbling up from the pit of her stomach, I am going to take her hand and force her to rent *Ford Fairlane*.

See how she likes the other side of the coin.

Middle-aged Loony

There was an extra at the TV show where I work, probably in her fifties. She wore brown bell-bottoms and a crocheted vest of many colors. She sported a jaunty hat. She decided to strike up a conversation with me.

"I'm a very big animal-rights activist, you know," she said.

"Aah," I said and ran away.

Women like this make me real nervous. They exude a kind of batty eccentricity, a purposeless desperation, an inane beside-the-pointness, a skewed inner vision that keeps them from making meaningful connections.

They can be easily recognized by their outfits, which are entirely schizophrenic: denim caps and beaded bags, sweatpants and chiffon. They always have some major scarf action around the head and neck, especially in L.A., where they seem to clog, and often bring to a halt, supermarket checkout lines.

In Manhattan these women can be found striking up conversations with waiters in Greek coffee shops, who don't have a clue what they're talking about but listen politely. Or in Korean markets, where they painstakingly count each penny to pay for two cans of Fancy Feast, then suddenly decide they also want Nilla Wafers.

You know these women. You see them on the street. You avoid them.

So do I. Which is why recently I went insane when I realized that any day now I will turn into one of them. Well, maybe not that soon. I'm in my early forties. That's not middle-aged anymore, is it? Okay, technically it is, but doesn't middle age start in the mid-fifties or maybe even later? And so what that I've gone all doggie? I only have four dogs, not fifteen or anything weird like that. (That I also have goldfish, with names, is a total accident.) And even if I become middle-aged, which I guess I probably will, that doesn't mean that I'll be one of those strange babes. Does it? I've always been part of the lunatic fringe, but I don't want to be an actual lunatic.

Oh, shit. Shit. I've just looked down at my clothes. I'm wearing paisley leggings with plaid shoes.

Okay, the thing is not to panic. No. The thing is to figure out what I'm panicking about. Why do these women frighten me? I mean, who are they?

They're casualties of the prefeminist society, when you had to have a man or you were an outcast. When any sort of self-sufficiency was frowned upon, when careers were verboten, these women had husbands who left or never appeared at all, children who grew up or never existed.

So these women, taught to rely on men, were left without re-sources.

We young people (shut up!) grimace and roll our eyes when they carefully count out those pennies ahead of us at the market, but perhaps these strange babes are not just trying to annoy us. Perhaps they're not buying Fancy Feast for their felines.

Because they've been abandoned by a society that has no use for them, that doesn't care whether they live or die, they've escaped into goofiness.

But this won't happen to me. Because I am a feminist.

Well, it could happen to me, because the feminism that I know omitted one important lesson: Expect nothing.

We get so angry with men! They treat us badly! Like sex objects! Like second-class citizens! We rail against their paternalism! Their condescension!

But how do we tell them? We wheedle and cajole like little wimps! We pout and get angry and argue and throw plates! We tell them incessantly how much it hurts us when they treat us badly, and if they don't listen we try to force them to listen.

I say if we expect something from men we're doing it wrong and are destined for failure and curdled disappointment. Because we're working from a position of weakness.

But if we really, in our heart of hearts, expect nothing, if we lay some elemental ground rules, if we only deal with men who have respect and empathy for us, and have no truck with those who want us to enter wet-T-shirt contests, if we stop getting angry at bad treatment but simply ignore those who treat us badly, we could be okay.

Meanwhile, I think I'll just succumb, grow loony gracefully. I'll be a postfeminist middle-aged maniac, the strange old bird with one hundred dogs wearing an old black leather jacket. Young people like I used to be will roll their eyes at me. Fuck 'em.

Dear Problem Lady:

Do I have to have an opinion about Thelma & Louise?

You know how you can't go to dinner, or to a party, or even to the corner to buy carrot juice without hordes of people running up to you and saying, "So, Thelma & Louise, *what about that ending, huh? Was it a feminist movie or what the hell was it? Was the violence okay or is it bad for women? What about role models? How could Thelma have done it with that guy right after that other thing happened to her? Do you think it was just rampant male-bashing? Was it Butch and Sundance? Were Thelma and Louise just like men only smaller? And how about that goddamned ending? Huh?"*

Well, I just never know what to say. I liked the movie, I thought it was funny. I especially liked it when Susan Sarandon tied those skinny rags around her neck, she looked very cool and tough and I plan to tie some rags around my neck in a nonchalant manner really soon.

But I have no opinion. Especially about the ending, because people refused to shut up about the ending even before the goddamned movie came out, so by the time I finally saw it I might as well have had electrodes attached to my head I was monitoring my feelings so closely. "What do I feel about this?" I kept asking myself as the car shot into the air.

I just don't know, okay? I just don't get all the fuss. Please give me an opinion so I don't look like a moron.

Sally

Dear Sally:

The reasons everyone's making such a fuss about Thelma & Louise *are:*

1. It's a really good movie.

2. Nobody can figure out why they haven't seen this movie before. Isn't this the kind of movie that we should have seen in the seventies?

Do American women need to be told that they don't need to ask their husband's permission to take a trip and leave him his dinner in the microwave?

No. But we're so used to seeing movies where the women play the love interests and get to say only these lines—

"Honey, come to bed, it's late."

"Honey, you've done all you could."

—that the very existence of Thelma & Louise has shocked us out of our movie stupor and now we're all overexcited. We've tasted blood, we want more.

But if you need to have an opinion, here's a suggestion. If someone tries to tell you that this movie is bad for feminism and that it provides terrible role models for women, remind them sweetly that men get to play all sorts of horribly complicated messes in movies whenever they want. Then pull out a gun and shoot them.

Problem Lady

Dear Problem Lady:

Can you tell me any tricks about not appearing desperate? People are always saying that a person can "smell" desperation. How can they smell it? What does it smell like? Does it smell bad?

It must smell terrible, judging from the way my mother and sisters talk about it. You should hear the pep talks they give me before I go out on a date:

"Don't forget to smile!" they say.

"You're just as good as anybody else!" they add.

"Don't forget to check your mascara," they advise. "Stand up straight!"

"Laugh at his jokes," they counsel. "Get your hair out of your face!"

I'm the only one who isn't married in the family, so I think they're a little desperate themselves. Sometimes they get on my nerves, but they mean well, they're just worried about me.

And who can blame them? I live alone in a bad neighborhood. I hardly make any money at my job (I work at an art gallery and paint on the side), and I haven't had anyone in my life since the spring before last, and that didn't work out. Now he's married to a nursery school teacher.

I tell them not to worry, the East Village is safe now, and if I don't find a man in the next year I'll move back to Queens with them and be safe and they can fix me up with whomever they want.

But with this desperation of mine, this smelly desperation, I don't know how I will ever find anyone to love, anyone who will love me, and I don't want to move home in disgrace.

The whole thing makes me so nervous my palms are always soaking wet. I go out on dates and I freeze up and I can't speak and my palms squeak. Their advice isn't working.

So is there anything you can tell me? Is there anything else I should know about hiding desperation besides smiling, checking my mascara (I have greasy skin and the mascara smudges easily), and laughing at his jokes?

Laura

Dear Laura:

I have something I want you to do for me: Buy a shotgun, go out to Queens, and hunt down your mother and sisters. Make sure none of them survives.

You think they love you and want what's best for you, but they're destroying you! They're making you into the scapegoat of the family so they can feel better about themselves! They have a big investment in your feeling desperate and unloved! I mean it! They're not well!

Okay, okay, I guess you can't shoot them. But please stop colluding in your own destruction. The most amazingly sexy stunning gorgeous bombshell in the whole universe would wilt and shrivel if she had people constantly clustering around her telling her to smile and laugh. Madonna (the singer, not the virgin) herself would begin to feel insecure and lumpy if people started shouting, "You're just as good as anybody else!" in her ear. Nobody ever says things like that unless they want you to believe the opposite.

You want to be a painter. But you're so self-deprecating you've put this gigantic part of yourself in parenthesis. If you didn't have this constant and supremely misguided pressure from your misbegotten family, becoming a painter would replace having a man as your first priority, you would be able to relax about men and get on with your art, and things would happen to you. You'd be able to have adventures instead of being paralyzed, which you are now.

Listen, you don't have to hate your family just because I do. But please don't listen to them anymore.

About desperation: It doesn't smell bad. Everyone who's lonely, everyone who wants love and closeness is "desperate." It's nothing to feel bad about, it's normal and odorless.

What stinks up the room is shame, and fear. When you think you don't deserve what you want, and when you're afraid someone might find out what a lowlife you are, you emit a putrid body odor that makes people run screaming in the other direction.

You're not a lowlife. Live in your lousy neighborhood and be creative and brave and let your family find something else to make them feel better about their empty little lives.

Problem Lady

Family Values

My Dog, Myself

Sally my dog is so nuts about me. She had a little something to do upstairs, probably growl at a plant she hates, and when she came back down she couldn't find me and she panicked. I saw her craning her head all around, then sniffing, then whimpering nervously before finding me right where she left me in front of the TV. She bounded over and collapsed at my feet. Half an hour later I looked down and there she still was, staring fixedly into my eyes.

I know where she's coming from. I too know the feeling of being totally obsessed.

I have decided that if you have a dog you don't need to read John Bradshaw books and find the child inside yourself. Having a dog means that the child inside yourself is made manifest in canine form.

Dogs do all the things we want to do but won't. Dogs act exactly the way we would act if we had no shame. I mean besides constantly licking their genitals.

We went for a walk today and there was a fat feisty little dog roaming free who bared her teeth at us. Then she started this mean, low growling. Then, barking and snarling, she charged. I put up a brave front. I yelled, "HEY!" Then I sprinted like hell. I want to be like this dog. I want to be fat and feisty and bare my teeth and have people go strange with fear and run away.

Last week I was at a party pretending not to notice a certain blond guy. I laughed, I chatted, I swiveled hither and thither vivaciously, pretending not to be clocking every single movement the blond guy made. It would have been a lot braver if I could have followed this guy around a little, if I could have worn my interest and insecurity on my sleeve instead of pretending I wasn't obsessed. There are big perils to acting like you're feeling one thing when you're secretly feeling another:

a. You exude dishonesty like a bad vibe.

b. The real feelings curdle inside you and you become twisted and strange.

So next time I see this guy I'm going to wag my tail and sniff his crotch.

Just recently I became temporary curator of another dog, Newton. Newton was abused as a puppy. Whereas Sally has always been treated like the queen of the world. The differences between them fascinate me.

You can tell how a dog is feeling by his tail. If his tail is up, he's happy, if it's down, he's unhappy. If he's wagging his tail, he thinks he might be happy but he's nervous about it. Newton, who was abused, is constantly wagging his tail in a tentative manner and putting his head under my hand to get petted. He needs incessant proof that I like him. Sally's tail is always up, never wagging, and although she will give affection when she's in the mood, she never *asks*. I identify with Newton.

One time I rolled up a newspaper and waved it at them, God

knows why. Newton whimpered and ran under the sofa. Sally thought she might bite the newspaper but lost interest.

The worst thing is that if you accidentally hurt Newton, step on his foot or something, he thinks he's been bad, he thinks it's his fault. He slinks up to you and tries to get you to like him again. This makes him the living metaphor for every adult I know who had abusive parents. Someone hurts you, you spend all your time trying to get him to love you instead of just keeping out from underfoot.

But in the park, Newton is intrepid and feisty, making dogs eight times his size play with him. Whereas Sally pastes herself to my ankles. Me in kindergarten.

(Right now they're both obsessing on a bee, following it, trying to bite it. Maybe we're not exactly the same.)

If I try to pat one dog, the other dog immediately starts a big game of rolling over on the floor and growling. The other dog will do *anything* to wrest away my attention. Jealousy! A biological imperative!

Some shrinks talk about how repressed hostility against mothers makes women competitive with each other. I would like to direct them to dog packs, to the dominant and submissive females, roles clearly choreographed. We are pack animals too. Our leader is Bill Clinton, ha ha.

Nondog people curl their lips and call dogs child substitutes. No, I have a child, it's totally different. Dogs are us, only innocent.

Dysfunctional Family Values

Do you ever feel as if you're living in two alternate universes at the same time? No? I do.

In one universe there's Mr. Potatoe-head, that oozing lump of vacant protoplasm, that dickhead who talks about the "cultural elite" when we know he means "Jews," that cow patty in human shape we recently called our vice president. It seems that this living definition of cretin has, with searing pointlessness, become the defender of "traditional family values." You can't shut him up.

This would be just fine except he seems to have struck a chord. We all have rosy memories of a simpler, happier time—a time of homemade apple pie and gingham curtains, a time when Mom understood everything and Dad could fix anything. "Let's get those fabulous traditional family values back!" we murmur to each other.

Meanwhile, in a simultaneous universe, everyone I know, and every celebrity I don't know, is coming out of the closet to talk about how miserable they are because they grew up in dysfunctional families.

Roseanne Arnold, my next-door neighbor, and about eight out of every ten people I meet have been sexually abused by a family member. Our country is teeming with damaged humans who swarm into twelve-step programs where everyone shrieks and sobs about how they were sexually abused by their fathers while their mothers looked on in a drunken stupor.

Oprah, Phil, Geraldo, and Sally Jessy would all be selling shoes in Altoona if it weren't for compulsively blabbing suicidal teenaged prostitutes from transvestite-father, drug-addicted-mother homes. PBS would be bankrupt if its fund-raisers didn't feature hours of John Bradshaw explaining to sobbing audiences how our families fill us with toxic shame and make it impossible for us to have anything other than lives of agony.

So, which is it? Are traditional family values saviors or destroyers? What are traditional family values, anyway?

Yesterday I sat staring into space for three hours, trying to think of one single traditional family value. Don't talk with your mouth full? Wear clean underwear in case you're in an accident? Get your hair out of your face? I just don't know.

Is it possible that those people on talk shows and in twelve-step programs, etc., are all Democrats? Could Quayle mean "Republican" when he says "traditional"?

Figuring that no family could be more seminal than the Reagans, I decided to pick up the new Patti Davis book to check.

I couldn't believe it! Patti and I had the same childhood!

Nancy took too much Miltown, Valium and Dalmane. So did my mom! Patti did all kinds of drugs in high school and her parents never noticed. Me, too! Nancy would pretend she was actually dying in order to guilt-trip Patti into obedience. Déjà vu! Nancy chopped off Patti's hair and made her wear dreadful clothes and Patti's dad would sort of dreamily ignore his daughter's misery. When Patti displeased her at social functions, Nancy would go sulk in the car. Patti was terrified of her mom, and couldn't connect with her dad. Ditto, ditto, ditto!

Okay, my mom didn't hit me daily and my dad was a pharmacist, not the president of the United States. But the intrinsic nature of traditional family values made Patti and me both grow up twisted and strange!

So now I've come up with a theory:

We've all had miserable and strange childhoods, which is why we all seem to share the same neuroses. One of these neuroses is denial.

In an effort to avoid our actual lives, we spent our formative years watching television. Those rosy memories we all share are actually memories from our favorite TV shows: We've confused our own childhoods with episodes of "Ozzie and Harriet," "Father Knows Best," and "The Brady Bunch."

In real life, Ozzie had a very visible mistress for years, Bud and Kitten on "Father Knows Best" grew up to become major druggies, and Mom on "The Brady Bunch" dated her fifteen-year-old fictional son.

But who cares? Television has become our reality, and reality has become our nightmare.

Condensed Diary of a Single Mother

1970: I don't think I can make it. The Lamaze breathing is use-less. I'm pushing, I'm panting, I'm screaming. "Just one more!" the doctor prompts. I give a mammoth push. It's a boy! A perfect boy! Too many babies are born at once, there are not enough recovery rooms. My baby and I are pushed into a hallway where I nurse him for two hours. The hospital has forgotten us, we are in our own little world.

1971: My baby walks, and talks, and laughs. My husband doesn't. He's depressed, I'm depressed. Mounds of dishes are in the sink. Yesterday I found a plate with an ancient half-eaten sandwich under the bed. My baby speaks in clear sentences, my husband and I speak entirely in baby talk. My whole life was one long preparation to be a wife and mother and now I am. But I can't get out of bed. This is all wrong.

1972: My parents hate me, my in-laws hate me, my husband is catatonic, but too bad. I took the baby and left and now I live with another mother in another town. Eve has two girls. I'm working and give Eve half my salary to care for the kids and run the house. She is, in effect, my wife (without sex). And I've joined a consciousness-raising group to find out about this newfangled Women's Lib. It seems I've been oppressed and thus depressed. But now I love working and coming home to a happy fed toddler. I love living the man's role. I love this feeling of optimism I have, that anything is possible.

1973: Spring. Eve has left me for some guy. I'm working two jobs, one to make a living, the other to pay for the baby-sitter. I come home from my day job, sleep for a couple hours, then cook at a gambling club all night. I'm so tired I cry all the time. My mother wants me to come home, live with her. Never.

1973: Autumn. Living with my mother makes me feel dull and colorless. She wants to shoehorn me back into the life I left, wants me to find a man to take care of me. I'm working as a temporary secretary. I meet a man, a freckle-faced med student. He asks me out. My mother is ecstatic. When I tell him about my child, his eyes glaze and he stares out a window. My kid is anxious and unhappy, I can tell. He wears his pacifier on a string around his neck. My mother wants me to take it away from him.

1973: Winter. New York! It's so cool! I'm living in a loft with my married friends Sam and Ellen and their baby. We're sleeping on mattresses on the floor and making art and working at home for an ad agency. The babies wear goofy colorful clothes and we take movies of everything they do. My son paints giant pictures and pretends he is a train and sings to me all day.

1974: January. I've been standing on the welfare line for three hours. My son is in the "nursery," twenty children trying to play with one truck. I have to pee but hate going into the toilets, they are filthy and have no seats. The welfare clerk is trained to treat welfare mothers like scum. I'm cringing with fear and shame when I get to the front of the line, which is just as well, because they will just send you away unless you have a full-blown sobbing fit. They haven't sent my check in a month, some problem with the terms of the lease on my dingy slum apartment. It's arbitrary, just to get me to give up and go away. I would go away but we need to eat, so I cry for ten minutes and finally get a check and some food stamps. I wish I could find a day-care center without a huge waiting list. I wish Sam and Ellen hadn't broken up and the ad agency hadn't gone out of business. I really wish I didn't believe the welfare people are right when they treat me like scum.

1974: February. My son cut his leg and within hours it turned into blood poisoning. We're in the hospital emergency room. He's very frightened, so I'm telling him an interminable story about the two of us being alone in a boat trying to reach a magical island.

1974: August. We're walking down the street, him to day care, me to work. He loves his day-care teacher, a gay man with long hair and many plaid shirts. I love my secretarial job, now I can afford a telephone and self-respect.

1975: So now he's in kindergarten, so I have to take him to school in the morning, leave work at three, run with him over to the day-care center, run back to work, run to the day-care center at five-thirty. I don't have a love life, but we have a TV.

1977: At one of those little alternative newspapers, the boss took a look around at all the single parents, realized how much time was spent running to and from child-care facilities, and hired a teacher. The teacher picks up all the kids after school and brings them to work: There's a big room with tons of toys and books. I love being lost in my work and then seeing my son's little round face appear over my shoulder.

1979: My son goes to visit my ex-husband's parents in the country for a summer of Little League and catching fireflies. I'm left on my own in New York to run amok. The first month he's gone, I catch myself every ten minutes thinking, Where is he? Don't I have to get home? Then I remember he's gone.

1984: I am a successful writer! We move from our tiny hovel to a huge apartment!

1985: My son gets into the High School of Music and Art, the *Fame* school. All his friends are funny and sane; all come from single-parent families.

1988: He goes away to college. I'm destroyed.

1989: I get a dog.

1992: I go on the "Tonight Show." "I was a welfare mother," I tell Jay. He's uncomfortable and quickly changes the subject before I can add, "And yet my kid just graduated from college magna cum laude and Phi Beta Kappa. Welfare mothers are persecuted and reviled for not working, even though only the rich can afford day care. Our country just loves punishing its victims."

1993: My son can't find a job and has moved back home. We're getting along great, although the little bastard could do a dish once in a while.

Mothers: The Bad and the Terrible

He hates me, I know. He wishes I were a million miles away.

"Why do you hate me?" I ask him.

"I don't hate you," he says with weary exasperation. He's said it about twenty times today. I'm really getting to him now. He's going to throw something at me in a minute. My rampant neediness is repulsing him. I'll try to stop myself. I can do it. No I can't.

"You hate me and you know it."

"Would you please shut up, Mom?"

Okay, yes, I'm horrible! I'm playing lame, guilt-tripping little games with my own kid! Which he definitely doesn't need! Which I'm only doing because I'm lonely, I'm in the middle of this transition of moving and totally changing my life, I'm scared to death and I have no man in my life to help me through this. So I'm taking all my weakness and fear out on my kid. Trying, in a sick and twisted way, to get him to take care of me!

Luckily he's not buying it.

There are excellent reasons for people to hate mothers. Mothers can be evil. Mothers, who oft can control nothing else, can control the actual minds of their children, can mold and shape them into any sort of sniveling beast they want. Mothers, who traditionally have little or no power in the outside world, have absolute power in their homes and over their children. Absolute power corrupts absolutely.

(This is a little scary. I originally wrote this for a magazine riddled with pictures of naked women. I, a woman, am saying women can be evil. Some feminists would probably scream at me. Women, they figure, especially in the midst of what some consider misogyny, should be portrayed positively. My feeling is that as long as women are not portrayed as stereotypes, as long as they're not portrayed as airhead bimbos or conniving temptresses or wide-eyed virgins in slow motion, I'm for it. There are the good guys and the bad guys in both sexes, and I was very happy to see Kathy Bates swing a sledgehammer and break James Caan's legs in *Misery*.)

I had a really exhilarating moment at a New Year's Day party. The guys were in one room talking careers, the women were in another room complaining about mothers. We had all just got back from Christmas with our families.

"I just couldn't *stand* my mother!" said Marsha. "My niece was wriggling around, the way little kids do, all excited, telling a story, and my goddamned mother says, 'Now couldn't we sit quietly, like a lady?' She did that to me when I was a kid! That's why I'm nuts!"

"My mother had to know where everyone was," said Mary Jo. "If someone even went into the bathroom, she had to know why and for how long. Christmas is her chance to be the boss of everybody again."

Pretty soon antimother anecdotes were flying around the room. We were giggling, having the best time.

"My mother seemed a little testy with me this time," I said tentatively. "For some reason I really got on her nerves."

"But that's not your real mother, is it?" Marsha said.

"Well, she's my ex-mother-in-law. We kind of adopted each other."

"But what about your real mother?" someone asked.

(I don't want to talk about my real mother. I just wouldn't know where to begin, I would get too sad. Okay, just one thing:

When my sister and I grew up, the deal in our family was that our mother was the monster and our father the hapless victim. She was crazy and abusive, while our father just stood around looking helpless, sheepish. "Poor Daddy," my sister and I would say to one another. "She treats him so badly."

But now as a grown-up, I see that they were involved in a passionately strange *folie à deux*. He had the power and pretended he didn't. She had no power and pretended she did by tyrannizing us. When we thought she hated us, she didn't even notice us, she was just railing against her own feelings of helplessness.

Our father is remarried now. "His new wife is so mean to him," said my sister recently. "Oh, come on," I said, "that's the way he likes to play it.")

Children are so often the victims of the insanity inherent in "romantic" relationships. Love might be real, but romance is ephemeral. Romance dies and Mom is still stuck with her brats. Some mothers are sensible enough to cope. But others are pissed off that they're not living happily ever, and guess how they take out their frustrations?

There is no such thing as a perfect mother, but I think good mothers are women who have self-awareness, who know how much power they have over their own children, who can discipline themselves against abusing this power. Good mothers, when they realize they're guilt-tripping their kids, stop themselves in mid-whine. Oh Jesus.

Bad mothers, as everyone knows, are the ones who sniffle and sigh, "All I want is for you to be happy." Bad mothers are the ones who sob and cry, "I just can't help myself!"

And the really evil mothers are the ones who think of themselves as victims, who think that everything that happens is somebody else's fault. The ones who take utterly no responsibility for their actions but always figure out a way to blame someone else. The martyr mothers.

(This is, of course, not just true of mothers. I have noticed that people who think of themselves as victims invariably fuck over everyone in their paths. They're so sure someone's going to do it to them that they get their licks in first. Hitler probably thought of himself as a martyr.)

The only way to get mentally stable kids is to have mentally stable mothers. This means women who have decent self-esteem, women who have control over their own lives and power in the outside world, not just in their own kitchens.

You know, women like me. My son's going out now. I wanted to go to the movies with him, it's his last night here. But no, Mr. College would rather be with his *friends*. I want to say "Don't leave me!" so much it's killing me. I'm going to. I open my mouth.

"Have a good time, hon," I say. Victory. For now.

Birth Control: The Facts

I can't even find my diaphragm anymore. Should the opportunity present itself, I've got some condoms stashed in the back of my underwear drawer. You have to be safe, and so I'm back where I started.

With condoms. Fourteen years old and gasping with terror, lying in the middle of a football field under my boyfriend. It's midnight and he's fumbling with . . . what? What's he unwrapping? Chewing gum? What . . . oh my God. This can't be happening to me. It must be someone else. This must be a movie.

I got used to the sound of ripping foil in the dark—in a stairwell during a night basketball game, in the playground of my elementary school, the building looming all white and eerie and subversive in the moonlight. Once even in the backseat of a speeding car. Wow.

But I never saw one. I didn't know what they looked like. Until one day I left the house to go to school, all scrubbed and carrying a million books, my hair shoved out of my face by a big barrette wielded by my mother (removed as soon as I hit the corner), when I saw something in the gutter and I just knew that shape. Just lying there in the gutter. And I realized what it was and where it had been and where it was now and I was sick and dreadful with shame.

Then when I was eighteen and living in one commune after another in crazed hippie fashion I went on the pill. We all did. And I bloated up and my breasts went all sensitive and globular and I wept bitterly at the drop of a joint. My mood swings verged on the psychotic.

"Why do all you girls burst into tears all the time?" my boyfriend complained.

"You don't love me anymore!" I whimpered.

"And you're all getting kinda chubby," he added.

"I will knife you in your sleep," I whispered.

What was it? The migraines, the constant nausea, maybe a threatened blood clot? Anyway, the doctor took me off the pill and inserted my first IUD. She called it a "coil" and it looked like one. Plastic and curly. She put it in my uterus.

"This will hurt a little," she said, and then there was an intense burning pain deep inside my belly until I blacked out for a second or two, and then I went home and to bed.

I'll always remember lying there in that room for two days, having menstrual cramps times ten, sweating and bleeding and staring stupidly at the ceiling. Occasionally some hippie or other would bring in iced tea and brown rice and wipe my forehead.

Then I got better and hardly noticed the IUD at all except during my period, when I was always certain I was hemorrhaging and about to die. But so what, I had lost all that pill weight.

Things were fine until I got pregnant.

"Don't be an asshole, I've got that IUD," I told the doctor.

"Don't call me an asshole," said the doctor, "babies have been born with IUDs clutched in their fists." And she showed me a picture.

So my boyfriend and I decided to get married.

"You've got to get down on your knees and ask me properly," I told him, and that sweetheart, he did.

The next day I miscarried. Because of the IUD. I was assured, as I went into full-throttle labor, that this was to be expected, it was very common. They took me to the hospital and gave me painkillers and my mother sat with me all night. I'd wake up and look for her. "I'm here, honey," she'd say. In the morning they scraped my uterus of debris and sent me home.

Well, we got married anyway. And I don't remember what we did. I think the famous coitus interruptus. I remember a lot of sticky stomachs. And then one night while doing it we whispered and decided he wouldn't pull out and we would have a baby. So we did, and I did.

I didn't need birth control while nursing, but eventually, on medical advice, I got another IUD, they were allegedly improved. This lasted through beginning parenthood, the breakup of my marriage, living for years in England, coming back, becoming a writer, falling in love, and becoming very, very ill.

"You've got a uterine infection, pelvic inflammatory disease, caused by the IUD," said the gynecologist. "It'll have to come out, but unfortunately it can't come out, somehow or other it's turned upside down and I'd have to operate."

So he gave me massive doses of antibiotics off and on for over a year because the infection kept recurring. I was lucky because I didn't have to be hospitalized. And finally the IUD decided to right itself, he took it out, and I tried contraceptive foam.

Which was delightful and fun, like filling your innards with whipped cream. And I got pregnant right away. My boyfriend wanted to kill me. He thought I did it on purpose. He was horrified at the thought of a baby, so I had an abortion. My gynecologist told me

Jewish American Princess jokes as he vacuumed out my insides. It didn't hurt much, just a few rampant twinges. What did hurt was that my boyfriend, still livid, took me home, put me to bed, snuck out to spend the night with an old girlfriend, and let me find out about it. And of course the nightmares about my dead baby.

Then my beloved gynecologist fitted me with my beloved diaphragm. At first I was afraid of it. At first I would smear it with spermicide and try to put it in and it would madly shoot across the room and land in the bathtub. Or I'd put it in wrong and discover I couldn't walk without intense agony.

But eventually I got the hang of it and it was fine. No pain. No strange bloatings. Just the feeling of constantly being awash with spermicide. Just wondering if the six hours were up and I could take the festering thing out. Just having to excuse myself and spend five minutes in the bathroom before every sex act. Just the yeast infections.

I'd heard the new pill is infinitely better. But my friend got pregnant with them. She had double vision, intense migraines, painful contractions. The doctor told her if the child was born it could have birth defects, and if a boy, somewhat feminized. I'm getting so tired.

Will there ever be a male contraceptive pill? What do you think?

The Baby Machine

Girls! Want to have a baby? No man in sight? Here's why it's hard:

Your body doesn't want you to. I recently read somewhere that our bodies are still geared for the Stone Age, that we have to jog and lift weights because our bodies still think that any minute now we're going to be running from a lion or hefting a dead seal on our shoulders, and we go to seed if we don't approximate these antics.

Our hormones, too, were formed back in the Stone Age, affecting our every thought. There were no Stone Age feminists. Women just didn't have the time for marches and petitions and legislation, they were too busy trying to discover fire. Therefore, when your modern self-actualized girl suddenly goes all goopy at the sight of minuscule Reeboks, her brain may well decide that it's time for motherhood. No matter that she's single and thirty-six; she has, after all, only one life. But when her brain informs her body of this decision, her body is shocked.

"Excuse me," her body snarls, "but where's the fellah? No way I'm going through nine months of intense vulnerability without a dude with a club to protect me."

At which point your modern girl feels a cold, heavy dread in the pit of her stomach, a dread which, freely translated, means that all the teensy Reeboks in all the world will never be enough to lead her to the turkey baster.

Take me (please). I became a mom when I was, I think, twenty, and never thought about it for a minute. One night we just thought, What the hell and moments later I had a wriggling infant attached to my breast.

For the past five years I've wanted another one, but there was never a guy. (Well, there *were* guys, but never the right guy.) And I kept trying to talk my body into it anyway—I would cajole, I would plead, I would threaten. My body was having none of it.

"You can't afford it, you don't have time for it," my body would inform me. I knew this was silly, since I have been a single mom half my life, early parts of which were spent in abject poverty. Now, when I am not working, which is often, I am lying on my couch reading fashion magazines. I can afford it, I have time. But my body remained aloof and unresponsive, it refused to entertain the notion, and I was stymied.

Well, not too long ago I met this guy. My body was ecstatic. "Okay, I'm ready now," it trilled, and released some powerful baby-making hormones that permeated every cell of my being; even my toenails demanded reproduction. I became all soft and thick-blooded and fecund, a walking zygote machine ready to happen. A new child seemed possible, probable, the most obvious thing in the world. I would happily have gotten pregnant at the drop of a skirt.

I know there is a chemical in chocolate that simulates the feeling of being in love (why couldn't it be in celery?), but so far no one has discovered the baby hormone in simple foodstuffs.

If you want to have a baby on your own, you have to fight your very nature. You have to steel yourself against feelings of futility and nausea. You must overcome every primitive instinct. This could be a brave move, or a foolish move. To decide, ask yourself these questions:

A. *Am I a trendy moron?* Many of us are, it's nothing to be ashamed of. Babies are hot right now. You know how you sometimes suddenly want a miniskirt, even with those knees of yours? Make sure your motherhood motivation isn't similar to this.

B. *Am I lonely?* Some women figure it's either a puppy or a baby. A baby is not company for you, you are company for it. You are also its servant, even if you have servants, until it is ten years old, when you may send it out to work in the fields. This is a horrible reason to have a baby—you will be even lonelier, since you can't just pick up and go out whenever you feel like it. You will end up hating your baby for all the misbegotten hopes you've pinned all over it. And it will end up on a psychiatrist's couch railing against your resentment and neediness.

C. *Do I want to play dolls?* If the only time you feel maternal is in the presence of the sweetest little antique christening dress with darling hand-sewn smocking, find a niece.

D. *Do I have an axe to grind?* "I won't do to my kids what my parents did to me" is moot motivation, because you will.

E. *Am I in throes of deep, abiding, and senseless maternal passion?* You'd better be, you'll need your strength. You'll have to tap every hidden stronghold of patience and responsibility. But it can be done. It's not nearly as expensive as they tell you, just steer clear of baby boutiques and designer schools. My kid wore thrift-store clothes, went to state-supported day care and public schools. He will probably become president.

And I love him more than life itself.

A Doctor in the House

Doc is feeling insecure today. He keeps climbing up on the bed and snuggling his head against my armpit. He keeps sighing mournfully. I stroke his stomach and he pretends to perk up just to make me feel better, but I can tell he's still unhappy, really. I wish he could tell me about his rotten childhood, but he can't, he's a dog. People tell me I'm just projecting when I say Doc is miserable or insecure. How do they know?

I first saw Doc while he was standing outside a pet shop, tied to a pipe, trying to get someone to adopt him. Big and black and sad, just standing in the rain. I was looking for a companion for my minute dog, Sally. Newton went back to his real human companion and Sally gets lonely if she can't smell another dog's butt at least thirty times a day.

"Who's that big black dog?" I asked Genora, the dog-rescue woman and my future friend. Genora has a dozen or so rescued dogs stashed in every area of her house while she desperately tries to find homes for them. On Saturdays she sits in front of the pet store with her dogs, hoping someone will fall in love with one or two of them. People from all over L.A. call her when they find a lost or abandoned or brutalized dog.

"Oh, that's Gibson, he's such a nice dog," she said.

"Too bad I want a little dog," I said.

I played with Buddy, a little black Shar Pei who had cigarette-burn scars all over his body and a bigger scar where someone had driven a spike into his leg. Buddy had been found wandering and damaged, he had been cuddled for several months, now he was loving and trusting, the fool. While Buddy licked my hand I felt a pressure against my knee. This big black Gibson dog was pressing up against me, mournfully. When I sat down, Gibson put his head in my lap. When I got up, he sat on my chair. He kept staring at me. His look said, plain as day, "You're the only one who understands me. I love only you."

When I left the pet store, Gibson was surrounded by children petting him. His eyes were half closed in ecstasy. I thought about him all week.

"Where did he come from?" I asked Genora.

He was a stray. A woman found him and put him in a kennel while she tried to find him a home. She had no luck. Big black dogs are a dime a dozen. Dog shelters are full of them, nobody wants them. Doc was in the kennel for six months. Genora saw him every day when she would visit her own surplus dogs. He was miserable. He had terrible diarrhea and was emaciated and severely depressed. She thought he was going to die and took him home.

I called Genora to ask how he was. "It's a shame I want a littler dog," I told her.

"I know," she said.

"Where is he now?" I asked.

"Oh, he's out on the patio, looking at a piece of rawhide."

"Is he okay?"

"He's a little lonely."

"Maybe he could just come and visit me for the weekend, I could cheer him up. I seem to have a special bond with him that nobody else has," I said.

"Okay," she said.

"Just for the weekend."

"I know."

He came for the weekend. Genora had bathed him and his coat was thick and glossy. He had the look of a child in his Sunday best—proud, hoping to be noticed, desperately trying to please.

During the weekend people came to visit. Gibson put his head in everyone's lap and stared up at them with a look that said, "You're the only one who understands me. I love only you."

"Gibson, you total slut," I told him.

On Sunday I called Genora. "You can't take him back, I'm crazy about him."

"Oh, thank God," she said.

I renamed him Doctor K after Dwight Gooden because of his soulful stare.

Sally pretends to hate him, but secretly, when I'm not around, they run around together. Sometimes when I come home I catch them playing tug-of-war. Sally pretends it never happened.

He's had one obedience lesson and now he sits and stays and heels and comes and is perfect, except for once in a while when he'll eat a book. Now that he's here, everyone wants him. People try to give me money. I tell them there are hundreds of wonderful dogs waiting at shelters. Dogs that stopped being cute little puppies so their owners just got bored.

"Is that what happened to you, Doc?" I ask him today while he presses against me and tries to curl into a little ball. "Were you somebody's little plaything? And then did you grow up and get all awkward and shy and artistic and didn't please them anymore?"

He has no idea what I'm talking about.

Dear Problem Lady:

Whenever my girlfriend comes over my cat, Basil, leaps into her lap with his claws unsheathed. He also lies between us all night, kneading the quilt, purring, jumping down, getting back up again. He even draped himself over my girlfriend's face the other night. She's getting a little testy.

Basil's other favorite trick is to fall madly in love with anyone who's allergic to him or just plain hates cats. He follows my poor friend Ralph around constantly. He jumps on the sofa next to Ralph and smashes his head on Ralph's hand, demanding to be petted.

I love the cat, but my girlfriend keeps hinting that I should get rid of him. Should I?

Rod

Dear Rod:

One doesn't make a commitment to an animal lightly. One doesn't take a fancy to an animal one day and have a whimsical change of heart the next. One adopts an animal for life except in severely mitigating circumstances. Or else one is scum.

Your coldhearted girlfriend can fend for herself. Basil can't, although he tries not to let you know it. And he can't help latching onto those who hate him; cats by nature are perverse. Get your stupid girlfriend to feed him and he'll leave her alone.

Just be happy he's not Louie, a Shih-Tzu I know. Every time Louie's master gets a new boyfriend, Louie makes a point of shitting on the boyfriend's side of the bed.

Problem Lady

Dear Problem Lady:

Isn't there a twelve-step program for people with absolutely no addictions whatsoever? We have pain, too, you know. We lie awake in the middle of the night agonizing over our loneliness and misery just as much as any addict, so why don't we get to share and say the serenity prayer? Why don't we get to use words like "enabler," "dysfunctional," and "denial"?

And why can't we nonaddicts have dates with the hundreds of unattached and desperately sensitive ex-alcoholics and drug addicts who stream through these meetings in a never-ending tide?

Okay, if you must know, yes! I want dates! I want romance, passion! I am the only one of my friends who's not seeing anyone! They're all in programs and their lives are all studded with lawyers named Tom, carpenters named Jeff, songwriters named Brendan. Especially songwriters named Brendan—there are a lot of Irish guys in AA.

So my pals are running off to romantic weekends in the country and I'm lying in bed eating Oreos.

Okay! Maybe I have an eating disorder! I do have a lot of trouble with Oreos and I do keep a bag of M & M's by my bedside or I can't sleep. But come on, is OA sexy?

And yes, I smoke! But I like smoking. I think I would be an alcoholic if I could, but when I drink all I get is kind of tired and headachy and sick to my stomach. Does this count?

Sometimes I take a Valium, but only like five a month. The occasional Vicodin I take for those headaches I get when I drink hardly seems serious. And I do have a Dalmane when I go on airplanes, but I don't travel that often. Pot makes me paranoid. Cocaine makes me mental.

I'm too selfish to be codependent. I don't gamble, I don't have debts, and even if I did have sexual problems I wouldn't go to SA—what kind of sicko guys would I meet there? I thought of Al-Anon, or ACOA, but my parents are teetotalers.

It doesn't seem fair that I have to endure my life alone.

Patsy

Dear Patsy:

It seems to me you could walk into the meeting of your choice with no questions asked.

Let's face it, you're awash with addiction. Eating, smoking, drugs—you may think you're a normal human, but to anyone in the program you're a mess. People in the program can find an addiction in the clouds in the sky. People in the program will embrace you and call you sister.

As far as I know, there is no meeting for the nonspecific addictive personality. A lot of them go to Al-Anon, but I have noticed that, unlike the other programs, people who go to Al-Anon often get worse instead of better. They act out, they preach, they go all sanctimonious. You don't want that, and you don't want a guy like that.

If I were you, I'd go to Smokers Anonymous, if there is such a thing, since you glossed over the smoking so quickly. But with all those pills, I wouldn't rule out NA.

Not only might you meet a guy, you might get better.

Problem Lady

Dear Problem Lady:

The world really truly unbelievably sucks. It sucks to the point where I can't even read newspapers and magazines without my stomach knotting. I can't bear to hear about the ozone layer. When I hear about the ozone layer, I have to go to bed. If someone tells me about the rain forests, I take a sedative right away. Then there's the elephants being killed for their tusks. And the owls dying to make way for loggers. And AIDS babies. And AIDS grown-ups. And children lying on little shelves for years in Romania, waiting to be adopted. And gorillas, and runaway homeless abused teenagers, and whales, and wolves, and Komodo Dragons.

And then there's just your everyday homeless people. There was a homeless couple on my street that lived in a doorway. Every night they'd put on pajamas, she'd put her hair in curlers, and they'd go to sleep on their cardboard bed. I felt so sad for them. I'd have little fantasies about what they talked about, what their childhoods were like. Did they squabble like I do with my boyfriend? Did she flirt with other men? Did he hog the cardboard when they were asleep? Was she from a little farm? Did his mother love him?

But what could I do? I couldn't give them a home or jobs. What can I do about any of this? It's all too much, too scary, too impossible, too overwhelming. Just while I was writing this, we lost 100 more acres of rain forest.

How are we supposed to live in this world at all?

Athena

Dear Athena:

Do the world a big favor and get over yourself.

You're so damned sensitive you've soured into sentimental. You're living in your own head and sound proud of your pain. Just stop it, nobody cares, they have too many other things to worry about.

So what that nobody can solve the world's hideous problems? Instead of imagining poignant stories, why not walk over to Woolworth's and buy that homeless couple a goddamned air mattress?

The trick is to just pick one thing. There are ozone activists. There are wolf activists. Be a drop in the bucket.

Don't go all delicate and foundering, too fragile to deal with the terror in the hearts of AIDS patients or the slack-jawed hopelessness of battered babies.

In the nineties we're all very tough and pragmatic and bored with hairdos, dresses, and the morbid state of our psyches. In the nineties we know that our world is corrupt and diseased but we're tired of being cynical and feeling helpless.

What the hell, tilt at a windmill.

Problem Lady

Dear Problem Lady:

My husband is always sick. Either his sinuses are killing him, or his head is pounding, or he's really nauseous, or he thinks he's coming down with the flu, or his throat hurts, or his chest hurts, or he has diarrhea, or his back is in spasm.

Yesterday he found it impossible to turn his head. We had to go upstate and I had to drive, and I'm a lousy driver.

"Pete, please drive," I said.

"I would if I weren't in such intense pain," he said.

"But you're always in some kind of intense pain or other," I said. I know that wasn't kind, but you don't have to live with him. If I've brought him one pill I've brought him a truckload.

"Thanks for being so supportive," he said sarcastically. And then we had this huge fight during which I accused him of being a hypochondriac.

"Take that back, Roeanne," he said.

"I do take it back," I said. "You're not a hypochondriac. You're a goddamned faker! Anytime there's something you don't want to do you find yourself a headache!"

He's been sleeping on the couch for a week. I don't really care, but that couch is really bad for his back.

Roeanne

Dear Roeanne:

Your husband isn't faking, he's on the verge of a nervous breakdown.

Everything you describe is a symptom of what fancy people call stress disorder.

Consider changing your approach. Your husband probably feels stupid and ashamed of all his aches and panics, which stresses him out even more. And then you give him shit.

Send him to a shrink, accept his complaints calmly, don't make him feel like a fool.

Because I'm not sure, but I think the next step is a heart attack. Oh, maybe I'm wrong.

Problem Lady

The Times

Big Brother Is Us

Every so often I grow despondent over my body and soul marching inexorably into middle age: I go to a nightclub and deeply inhale the heady odor of tobacco, whiskey, dirt and hormones, then after fifteen minutes I get tired and go home. I go to the drugstore to get stronger magnification reading glasses so I can read the cholesterol content of pretzels. I actually contemplate, for seconds at a time, pension funds. This can be devastating.

But then I remember that I rule the world.

Baby boomers are the chosen people. Our interior lives echo life in our country, life on our planet. The world was created as a favor to us. The rest of you, eat your hearts out.

First and most important, we got to be teenagers in the sixties. And you poor souls who are too young or too old have no idea how great it was to be young and fresh and full of hope and idealism when society was ditto, when anything could and did happen, when there was plenty of money and plenty of music.

I mean we could just walk into any record store and ask, "Can I please have the new Beatles album?" and they would hand it right over. *Rubber Soul, Revolver, Sergeant Pepper,* whatever. New Stones singles were constantly broadcast over the airwaves, along with all those new groups like The Who, The Doors, The Kinks, The Mothers of Invention, Jefferson Airplane, The Grateful Dead. Bob Dylan. Janice and Jimi. You call it "the classics" now, but we were there, they were there, it was a big party, everybody was invited. Who knew we were hanging with the equivalent of Beethoven and Mozart?

Instead of the fashion magazines, *we* decided how everyone should look, and then collapsed into giggles when our mothers wore miniskirts and our fathers let their hair grow long.

Plus we got to sleep with everyone we saw and got away with it scot-free. Maybe we got a couple of crabs. The pot, the speed, the acid? Maybe we got a little stupid.

Of course we single-handedly created the seventies. We started with Women's Liberation, and didn't even get tired. We went on to a fierce contemplation of our navels and got Tom Wolfe to call it the "Me Decade." We needed to do this, we were reinventing ourselves at such a dizzying pace. All those cultural, political and sexual revolutions left us insecure and confused.

Then we picked ourselves up, dusted ourselves off, and changed the face of media: Journalism, movies, and even television pandered to our new consciousness.

Then we got sick of all the life-affirming stuff and went all nihilistic and decadent. We invented punk rock and nightclubs. Not nightclubs where ladies wore chiffon and gentlemen wore suits and there was a lovely floor show; nightclubs where our clothing was held together with safety pins and we went to sadomasochistic balls and listened to the Ramones, Patti Smith, the Talking Heads, and yes, rap started then.

The eighties weren't our fault.

We were sitting on beer crates in the basement at God knows what after-hours club, out of our minds on a finely tuned combination of cocaine and Quaaludes, when young whippersnappers in their twenties and the old farts who'd been gunning for us since Vietnam banded together and wrested the times away from us. It was just terrible. We watched those little kids with their suspenders and cigars cozy up to Ronald Reagan and his pals and form an evil coalition of money-worshiping swine. We sat there drooling and helpless as the world we had so carefully crafted was raped and pillaged, never to be whole again. Our rage was frustrating, impotent, all we could think to do was have babies, order turtlenecks from catalogs, and invent a million new variations of the twelve-step program. And wait.

We waited. We got older.

Many baby boomers had hit forty when the bottom dropped out. When those of little faith who had forsaken us came streaming back into the fold, we were ready.

Is it any accident that as we hit middle age, a time when mortality becomes tangible, when terror strikes a soul because the end is in sight, the same thing happened to our planet? I don't think so.

Just as we are, our planet is hurtling toward destruction. And who're you gonna call to fix it? Us. Silly old us with our bell-bottomed minds and patchouli-scented souls will shoulder humanity's heaviest burdens. It's up to us to restore the rain forests and the ozone layer, to clean the air, to save the animals. Because we are the grown-ups now. We've put one of our own into the highest political office. We've always had the numbers, now we have the power.

If only we hadn't taken so many drugs, we might be able to handle it.

She Asked for It?

Who's this?

"Good morning, good morning, good morning, nice tits, good morning, good morning, good morning, good morning."

Justice Clarence Thomas greeting his Supreme Court colleagues, of course. You probably heard it already.

The most interesting part of those hearings was that the Democratic senators believed Anita Hill and the Republicans were convinced she was lying. That means none of them gave a shit; they were simply acting out of expediency.

Actually, I couldn't stand watching it all; it made me twitch and shriek to see the incessant, self-serving dishonesty. To have it thrown in our faces that our government is composed of morally bankrupt red-faced farts whose every gesture reveals their greed and stupidity. Even the Democrats suck. With the exception of Daniel Moynihan and maybe one or two others, they're all part of the biggest and grossest of the old-boy networks, and if a woman dares show her face among them, she is treated with patronizing courtliness or snickered at and dismissed (which is the same thing).

Anita Hill was portrayed as a lying floozy, powerless over her deep need to exact revenge on the man she couldn't have. Excuse me, but this is a woman in control. A black woman who has become a law professor is not powerless over any part of her psyche. This is not a woman scorned. This is a woman pissed.

But she became a pawn and ridiculous, and now women across the country are feeling their feminism rise again like a phoenix.

Almost every woman alive has been subjected to some form of sexual harassment. Here's personal testimony:

I was very young, just married, just started writing. And I got to interview the Who. Very thrilling! I went to their hotel. Keith Moon was goofy, John Entwistle quiet, Roger Daltrey boring and self-satisfied. Peter Townshend was wonderful. We talked for hours, about everything. I was in heaven. I was the coolest girl in the world!

As I was leaving, walking to the elevator, Roger Daltrey rounded a corner, saw me, and pushed me up against the wall. He smashed himself against me and whispered with his face almost touching mine, "Wanna come back after the show and give us all blow jobs?"

It doesn't seem like a big deal to me now, just some history without emotional resonance. But, back then! I got dizzy. I got sick to my stomach. I felt dread, shame, misery, overwhelming humiliation. There's no logic to it. I had heard the phrase blow job before. Why didn't I simply think, What an asshole?

Because at the core of my being, I thought it was my fault. I thought I had done something, who knows what, that showed I was a dirty girl who deserved it.

Sexual harassment is not about sex. Sexual harassment is a power trip. It's men taking revenge on women. Because they can. Because they're angry.

It happens all the time. The only women who don't believe that sexual harassment is a real problem in this country are women who have never been in the workplace. I'll never forget sitting in a dough-nut shop once, watching the manager interview prospective wait-resses. He wore his power like an obscene badge, humiliating and frightening every young girl who applied for the job. He got a real kick out of himself; he felt like a big shot.

There is the argument that sexual harassment happens primarily in blue-collar situations, where the men themselves are so powerless and frustrated that they need to find a scapegoat to make their misera-ble lives slightly better. But I work at a movie studio in Hollywood with a lot of educated, affluent people and, believe me, some very big-shot guys proposition, fondle and threaten young women on a daily basis. These young women have no power, they need their jobs to live, they're afraid to retaliate.

How are the powerless to retaliate? Go to court? The powerful have all the hot-shot lawyers.

But what I really need to know is, why does this happen so often? Why are so many men so angry at women? Why do they abuse women whenever they have the chance?

"Why is it?" I've asked my friends.

"I don't know," said my friend Paula. "I'm so used to male anger. It's been around all my life. The sky is blue, men are angry with women."

I asked my shrink. "They say it's a mother thing," he said. "That abusive guys are afraid of being restrained by their mothers, and this makes them hostile to all women. But who the hell knows?"

Virginia Woolf wondered the same thing. In *A Room of One's Own,* here's what she decided: "Women have served all these centuries as looking glasses possessing the magic and delicious power of reflecting the figure of man at twice its natural size. . . . [Men] say to themselves as they go into the room, I am the superior of half the people here.

. . . Take [this looking-glass vision] away and man may die, like a drug fiend deprived of his cocaine.''

In other words, men hate women because they need women to define their self-image.

I say that men also hate women because they desire them. This is where the sexual element comes in. A man is trained from childhood to be totally in control. His feelings are not important. His strength, his mastery over these feelings is all that matters. No crying, no neediness, or he is drummed out of the men's club. (By both men and women. Women can be more exacting about a man's behavior than men ever are.)

But a man can't control a woman he desires and he can't control his desire. Oh, he'll try. But he'll fail. And when a man is scorned, a man is pissed.

Woody, We Hardly Knew Ye

The nation is reeling. We are sleepless and dazed, crashing into walls. The country's morale has never been lower. A pillar of our existence has collapsed. Our hero has destroyed himself in front of our horror-stricken eyes.

Woody, what could you have been thinking?

Maybe it was a setup. There are two kinds of people in the world: those who think Woody Allen is the genius spokesman of our collective angst, and those who think he's a filthy Jewish liberal gay-sympathizing cultural-elitist Communist madman. Another name for those two groups are Democrats and Republicans.

So I'm thinking the Republicans have something on Woody or maybe put a horse's head in his bed, because the timing is just too perfect. Right in the middle of the Republican convention, during a huge orgy of family-values hysteria, suddenly this. The Republicans figure that all Democrats will become so disheartened, so depressed, so disoriented by the fall of their hero that they'll just shoot themselves. And if they don't shoot themselves they'll be too demoralized to vote. This theory could be true. Woody himself said that politicians are "a notch beneath child molesters."

I personally have new lines on my face. I looked in the mirror just now and two furrows have appeared since yesterday.

Yesterday wasn't too bad. Yesterday was the day the news hit. Everybody's first impulse was to laugh it off.

"I just want to say," said this comedian I know, "that Woody Allen became my hero when I was in junior high, he's been my hero all through my life. So I'm not just latching on now."

Yesterday we had your traditional fight between men and women, with the men swallowing hard and then maintaining how cool it was, and the women sullen and snippy about yet another man turning out to be just a stupid git who cares more about youth and beauty than grace and spirit, another man who discards his mate for someone one-third his age.

"Come on, we'd all do it if we could," said a waiter.

"He's an asshole. I hate him," said a waitress.

But today the reality has sunk in. Plus there is the story of child abuse and criminal charges, not that anyone believes he abused those tiny children, but still, the ugliness! Then we saw Woody being ever so Woodyish during his news conference. (This has nothing to do with anything, but could men like George Bush, Paul Shaffer, Warren Beatty, and Woody please stop covering their gray hair with that cheap reddish brown hair-color stuff? It's ugly and an insult to our intelligence. Guys, go to a professional.)

Seeing Woody's face and hearing that familiar voice made us realize that this wasn't just a fun show-biz scandal about people we don't give a shit about like, oh, Rosanne's singing or Liz's drug abuse, this was about our beloved Woody. A man who shaped the way we think, a man we identify with, a man we believe we actually know. But humiliating your mate by falling in love with her daughter, a girl you've known since she was nine years old, is something we don't want to know.

I'm worried about my son. This is a kid who has seen *Annie Hall* fifty times and can quote anything in any Woody movie verbatim. A kid who after seeing *When Harry Met Sally* astonished me by listing the dozens of scenes that were Woody Allen rip-offs. A kid famous for not reading, who's never read a single book of mine (the little bastard) but who has read all of Woody's.

"It's his own tragic fate," says my kid.

"Total self-destruction that great artists are prone to," I said.

"I guess I could see the signs but didn't want to," he said.

We had lunch today with my friend Alan the director. "I feel betrayed," Alan said. "He's the father, the power in the relationship. He has a moral responsibility. I keep thinking of that scene in *Manhattan* where he's standing in a schoolroom with Michael Murphy and a hanging skeleton."

"Oh, yeah," says my kid, "where he points to the skeleton and says, 'It's very important to have some kind of personal integrity. I'll be hanging in a classroom one day and I want to make sure that when I thin out I'm well thought of.' "

A bearded man at the next table leaned toward us and spoke. "It's an issue of such complexity that a novelist should deal with it instead of a judge," he said. "This country has just gone into totally surreal black humor."

The woman sitting with him piped up. "Love is blind, but Woody, hon, get yourself a seeing-eye dog!"

"And anyway," said Alan, "he's got final cut, what more does he want?"

The Great Telephone Answering Machine Conspiracy

This answering machine business is breaking my heart.

Remember when they worked? Even, oh, say three years ago, when *Consumer Reports* decided that the Panasonic 1424 was the best. But Panasonic will not sell us the 1424 anymore, now we've got evil machines, with or without the robotic time/date stamp, that want to drive us to suicide.

In the past three months, I've had three answering machines. The first one decided it hated my message and would only play it on Tuesdays. The second one would let me know from my remote location that I had messages but refused to play them for me, ever. The newest one (you won't believe this but it's true) suddenly has someone else's voice on it. A woman named Julie, and she and Herbert are not home. I don't know how this happened but I think I'm in the Twilight Zone.

It's not just me. I was at my friend Sonny's the other day. His machine broke utterly, and it had to be sent to Tokyo to be fixed. So he called up all his friends to find a substitute and we all brought over our answering machines from our own individual answering machine graveyards and no one brought less than three and no machine was older than a year. I sense a conspiracy. It could be the Japanese.

The entire fabric of our lives was transformed when we all got answering machines in 1976. *We could leave the house whenever we wanted to.* Then, while still giddy with our new freedom, we got to beep in and check our messages from afar. This meant that *we could stay away for days or weeks and still know everything.* I could be at Studio 54, and Stephen could be at the Mudd Club, and I could leave a message saying I was going to the Market Diner at four A.M., and he could check his messages and then call my machine and say to be sure and wait until five A.M., because he got a message from Greg who said he was in love with me and would Stephen meet him at five A.M. to discuss it. Okay, so then I'd have to go home and change, but not to check the machine.

And then the bliss of listening to see who it was! And having the machine stop the moment I picked up the phone instead of having to streak into another room to turn it off! And toll-savers! Room monitoring!

But it's all gone, maybe forever. My friend Teri's old workhorse Code-A-Phone finally kicked its heels in the air after seven years, and the guy at the shop told her, "Get it fixed, the new ones self-destruct the moment you get them home."

So if it's the Japanese, are they simply trying to take over the world? Will they soon own all the movie companies and every building in Manhattan and have us all foaming at the mouth at appliance stores, grabbing innocent salespeople by the throat? Will we soon be sleepless and unable to work and finally will we fall into a stupor while they take our jobs, move into our homes, wear our dresses, and rename our dogs?

But how evil can a foreign power be? More evil than our own phone companies? I think not.

Just as answering machines became untenable, phone companies have come up with their own incredibly expensive alternative! Coincidence?

For $80 million a month, the phone company will give you a number you can call, and a code. When you call that number, you have to punch in your own number, then you punch in your code, and then a few more totally random numbers until they finally relinquish your messages. It's very complicated, and I know many people who have tried this method and now they're sitting in darkened rooms and they can't stop crying.

But eventually we will all have to pay the $80 million a month and take night courses to master this method. And we will all heave a great sigh of relief and go back to having lives, not realizing that *the phone company has access to all of our messages and can do whatever it wants with them!*

And maybe the phone company will decide who's undesirable. Maybe the phone company, being big and faceless and basically malevolent, is in league with Jesse Helms. And the right-to-lifers. And gigantic corporations that pollute the earth and deplete the rain forest. Maybe the phone company is directly involved with the laboratory testing of animals.

And you know there will be some strange and twisted bitter man who will listen to all our messages. This man will find out that I'm prochoice, pro–animal rights, and a slut. He will erase all my messages from agents, from editors, from men, from dogs. Pretty soon all my income will have dried up and I will be a lonely, sex-starved bag lady.

I don't think I'm being alarmist. I think it's time to arm ourselves to the teeth and take to the streets.

Rich People: Blow Me

There I was in County Sligo, Ireland. This is Yeats country—teeming with tranquil lakes, hallucinogenically green. I was staying in a castle/ hotel. I should have been having the time of my life, but no. I was alive with hatred. Hatred for the hotel owner, a pear-shaped little snot in an ascot whose family, he swore, had owned the property since the actual dawn of time. But even more I hated all the rich morons swarming through this fucking castle.

They were pathetic. They all wore these tweedy, self-conscious little outfits, they all moved in that studied way of people who fancy themselves as elegant, they had greedy little eyes and chinless little faces, they talked with loud, self-important brays, their noses were perpetually out of joint, and giant logs were shoved up their butts. They exuded the stench of entitlement.

"The thing is," I said to my friend Ed, "they actually believe they're better than everyone else. And they're really thrilled about it."

"I want to take my penis out right now," Ed whispered, "just casually flip it out." Ed was doing a magazine piece about several places like this and invited me along and here we were, sitting in a drawing room in front of a fire randomly hating everyone we saw.

"Do it, please do it," I said.

"I want some tea!" barked a rabbit-faced fuck to a scared teenager in a uniform.

"Yes sir, right away," said the teenager and scurried off.

"What an asshole," said Ed. "Okay, I'm gonna do it."

He stood up, pulled his shirttails out, and secretly removed his penis and balls. Then he casually meandered around the room.

It was the most fun we had in Ireland (except for one time when we met this really nice dog). We got to the point where we would go to these fancy places, hang around in the kitchen with the help, and hide at the sight of other guests.

Rich people are pompous. Rich people are deluded. Rich people have to tell you every moment of their lives how rich they are. Rich people are stingy, coldhearted, mean, cowardly, immoral, furtive, dishonest, arrogant, petty, backbiting, ruthless, and pointless.

Well, maybe some of them are okay. The ones who came by their money inadvertently by doing something they really like, and some lost souls who inherited money and give it to weird performance artists can possibly be allowed to live. But mainly they're a scourge.

And here's the thing: It's not their fault. Rich people would be perfectly fine if we would all just stop sucking up to them.

We're all so busy trying to pry a little loose change out of them, trying to get them to buy this painting, that car, this precious little Ming vase. They start really thinking that maybe they are just too fabulous. And the more money they make, the more Porsches they buy, the more people seem to adore them! Rich people desperately want to believe their own press, they need so severely to think they are one of the chosen. This is what turns them into monsters.

I know this rich Hollywood TV producer who decided she wanted to be a singer. She decreed she would have a lounge act at a club. She wore lipstick an inch thick, a spangled tube top, and chiffon harem pants and croaked out Cole Porter numbers. It was a toss-up whether to watch her or kill yourself. But everyone who was in the TV business or who wanted to be in the TV business came to hear her. This includes every journalist in L.A., all of whom have sitcom pilot scripts in their glove compartments. So our chanteuse got rave reviews and was told by everyone how incredible she was. But after a couple of nights the TV people left and the regular people arrived. And then the overripe fruit started flying.

Now this TV producer is an utter monster. But once she was a normal person, and there is still a normal person trapped in there somewhere. And this normal person, like all normal people everywhere, is riddled with insecurity and self-loathing. When people suck up to her, her ego is massaged, but her soul knows it's a con. Her soul knows we only like her for her money and her ability to get us jobs. This makes her hate us, then herself. This makes her feel empty and alone.

After they threw the fruit at her, the TV producer went out and bought herself a Ferrari and a beach house, then fired the entire staff of a TV show. Rich people only trust money.

I say we stop this sucking up and treat them with the contempt they deserve. They have all the money, what more do they fucking want? And if we treat them really, really terribly, they'll really, really like us, and start showering us with money!

My Theory of Evolution

There are people, I hear, who think that human beings are the crown-ing achievement of evolution. That we are the supreme species, divinely created in God's image. That the buck stops here. I say get outa here.

Human beings leave a lot to be desired! We don't know enough to come in out of the rain!

Consider humans. We are stupid and self-destructive, a species in denial. We foul our nest to the point where it will soon be uninhabitable and then pout at the suggestion we should give up our Aqua-Net, our Huggies. We forget to educate our children. We're constantly reinventing miniskirts.

Clearly, there is room for improvement. And I personally have been waiting an awfully long time for the next step up the evolutionary ladder, for some kind of new, superhuman species that will put our petty, hopelessly addled species in the shade.

I've wondered how this species would manifest itself. Would it be a four-toed creature who never got fat even if she lay around all day eating bonbons and reading magazines? Maybe a creature born with an innate knowledge of quantum mechanics who never even cares if a guy calls or not? Or what?

For a long time, nothing. I know evolution takes forever, but this was getting ridiculous. If anything, humanity was getting stupider. We used to have fellows like Mozart running around! Galileo! Da Vinci! John Lennon! Plus a lot of women who were even smarter only no one let them read or leave the house! Now we've got, like, Madonna and Arsenio.

But you know what? I've been barking up the wrong tree, as it were. The change is nigh! It's happening even as I type this!

There is one thing that humans strive for with every cell, every gene, every nerve fiber of our beings. No, not being more intelligent. Humans hate being smart, it makes us think about things, and if we think about things for more than a minute we become incurably despondent. What every one of us wants is communication, connection, never being left out, never being alone on a Saturday night or ever. More than Mallomars, more than hot sex, we want to belong.

And so we've created the most incredible technology: It started with the printing press and the mail and now we're exploding with faxes, modems, fax-modems, voice mail, computer networks, overnight delivery, smart phones, television satellites and cable TV with five hundred channels. Pretty soon we're supposed to get teeny computers implanted in our heads.

But I don't think we need to. I believe in my soul we're finally on the verge of realizing our dream: We're becoming telepathic. Mass consciousness has become stronger than individual consciousness. Everywhere in the world, we're all thinking the same thing.

We have no choice. We may have fifty and soon five hundred TV channels, but they all show us the same images: A bunch of press guys surrounding the marines at Somalia, and Amy Fisher. We're all wearing at least one article of Gap clothing at all times. We've completely digested every aspect of the aesthetics of grunge.

And these all-pervasive images, these Gap T-shirts, this grunge-awareness has caused a weird mirroring effect on our actual brain pans, causing them to, well, mutate. Our thought waves are now colliding in midair. Communism toppled because the Russians wanted Air Jordans. In 1992, every living screenwriter was compelled against her will to write a movie with a blind protagonist. And, funnily enough, it turns out that everyone has simultaneously discovered that we are victims of child abuse.

We are one. The force is with us, finally.

Okay, so there's a bit of a downside. Originality may become extinct. Genius needs a dark, festering secret place with plenty of solitude in order to grow and flourish. Expose genius to the world prematurely and it shrivels up and becomes Milli Vanilli.

What would happen if Mozart were alive today? After composing his first symphony at the age of four he would be *Time*'s Man of the Year. He and his family would move to the Malibu Colony. He'd host "Saturday Night Live." He'd sign with Michael Ovitz, who'd package a sitcom for him. It would fail, as all sitcoms do, and little Mozart would go on drinking sprees and end up in rehab. At the age of, say, seven, Mozart would be a regular on "Hollywood Squares."

So no more Mozarts and no more counterculture. Counterculture needs a little pond far from the mainstream, but little ponds are immediately absorbed by the E! network scouring the world to discover random trends before they exist. Even without E! we would all intuit the little pond and quickly construct adorable waterside condos.

But hey, so maybe we'll be boring instead of self-destructive. And everyone will be one of the gang. I can't wait.

How to Be Creative

Do you ever get to wondering why certain things are so _bad?_ Why movies and television and magazines don't catch your fancy or make you sweat with enlightenment? Why everywhere around you people and things seem to be catering to some mythical consumer, some strange beast of a person who is exactly like you only completely stupid? Are you discouraged by incessant blandness? Would you like to take popular culture in your fist and smash it against a wall?

Me too! It's all I think about! (When I'm not thinking about sex, which I only think about very late at night and oh, in the morning and at dinnertime.) And here's what I think: I think humanity is vastly underrated.

We live in a dark and fearful time, a time of polls and ratings and market research. Polls and ratings and market research are an insult to everyone's intelligence, and are directly responsible for nobody wanting to read magazines or see movies anymore.

Many magazine editors and publishers wander around thinking, What do people want? They take polls, do research. They find out what people want, and give it to them. This doesn't work, since when people find their alleged ideas thrown back at them on glossy pages, these ideas are somehow changed, diluted, not what they meant at all. Sure, they're kind of interested in chicken recipes and Jerry Seinfeld, but really they already know that stuff, it's the same stuff they told the market researcher, it's boring. A person reads a magazine to learn; instead they find what they already know.

Television! People in Des Moines are not stupid! They have a taste for unconscionable desires and subtle irony! Many TV producers have a clear picture of TV viewers: morons who work in factories and who will buy Charmin toilet paper because Mr. Whipple is so trustworthy. This is never true! So writers submit scripts, then network execs say, "No, no, no, too goofy, too weird, it will never play in Peoria, rewrite it, make it more like 'Roseanne.' " We viewers end up trying desperately to identify, because that's what we always want to do in drama, identify with a protagonist who has the soul of a newt.

Movies are in the hands of businessmen who don't know they're businessmen! They fiddle with scripts, they second-guess the director, they hire market research people to make random phone calls to unsuspecting homebodies who suddenly have to decide whether *Autumn Idyll* or *Fire in the Groin* would be the better title for a Tom Cruise vehicle.

These people, these producers and editors and executives, are having trouble perceiving mass consciousness, and they think this is their job. Are they living in a narcissistic dream world? Has their contempt and cynicism taken over? No, they live in fear.

Everybody lives in fear. We all think we're incredibly weird and depraved and bonkers, and if people knew the real us they'd squirt acid in our faces and make us live in a Canadian mental institution.

But in fact, no matter how weird and depraved and bonkers we are, the guy next to us is just as strange. The truth about mass consciousness is that it is the very weirdness, the eccentricities and forbidden lusts in our souls that bind us together. (I think this is why the movie *Aliens* was so popular—we all think we have a monster like that living in our stomachs.)

There is only one way to be creative, and that is to have the courage to examine all our inner ripples and horrors and jokes and transform them into art. The hell with what the other guy thinks! The hell with the faceless populace, they can take care of themselves! The odder and more personal we get, the more everyone identifies. It's magic.

That's why big hits (later Sylvester Stallone movies notwithstanding) are never fashioned by committee. Big hits are made when the creators have courage, and the power to implement that courage. Roseanne isn't trying to please anybody but herself, it's her very weirdness we tune in for every week. When silly Stallone first started, he wrote a screenplay straight from the heart, complete with endearing goldfish. No committee would ever think of goldfish.

You want to create, go out on a limb. Go after editors who know what they like and the hell with the statistics. Go after producers who know they only know about money and don't try to fuck with your work. Don't listen to anybody, don't copy anything. Go after that twisted deranged core of your being, wrench it into the light, and you will make one million dollars.

Dear Problem Lady:

So like everybody we watched the Republican convention and this has nothing to do with anything but how do those Republican women live with themselves dressing like they do? I mean I know that the Republicans are trying to bring back the sixties and make it us against them, the hippie-gay-lesbian-feminist-liver-in-sin vs. the God-fearing-pornography-fearing-everything-fearing traditionalist, but to me it is a war between the chic and non-chic. But I digress.

So my boyfriend Eric and I watched the Republican convention, and like on the second day he said he didn't actually hate Pat Buchanan's speech.

"What do you mean, not hate?" I asked. "Not hate as in liked?"

"Well, no," he said, "I wouldn't say I liked it. It was just that one or two things he said kind of maybe made sense."

"Like what? Like antigay stuff? Antiwoman stuff? What, exactly?"

"Oh, I don't know. Pretend I never spoke."

I can't pretend he never spoke. I keep at him. Last night while he was talking in his sleep (he always says "Not windows! Banana!") I whispered in his ear, "What do you like about Pat Buchanan?"

"Banana!" he screamed.

It's just nagging at me. I mean, I'm sure there must have been something decent that Pat Buchanan said, right? Something okay and normal, but he makes me so spitting mad I can't for the life of me think what it could be.

I'll probably forget about it if I put my mind to it, but I feel something has come between Eric and I.

Suze

Dear Suze:

Something has come between you: a yawning, bottomless chasm that can never be transversed. It may look like just a teeny crack to you now, but believe me, it will widen until, twenty years from now if you and Eric are still together, you will have become one of those horrible couples you sometimes see in restaurants. You know the ones: Both parties look like they've sucked a lemon, they never talk or even make eye contact, you can feel their mutual loathing at fifty paces.

There is no way that a person who likes anything about Pat Buchanan can happily share a life with someone who hates him. The man is the nineties' version of a fascist.

(Every decade has its fascist movement: In the sixties the fascists were the idiots who wore American flags in their lapels and buttons proclaiming, "Boys! Keep America Beautiful! Get a Haircut!" In the seventies the fascists were the Est people, the ones who believed that everything that happened to you was entirely your own fault, which, when you take this philosophy to its natural conclusion, means that the Holocaust was the Jews' own fault. In the eighties the fascists were the crazed greedy cigar-smoking suspender-wearing money guys. And now there are the people who talk with a straight face about traditional family values, the ones who kind of like something that Pat Buchanan once said.

I know you're thinking what every woman thinks when her relationship hits a snag, but trust me, therapy won't help this guy. Nor will he grow out of it. As he gets older he'll get even more conservative, we all do.

Make a clean break right now. You'll thank me in the end.

Problem Lady

Dear Problem Lady:

I am simply furious with all the people who want to save the rain forests.

It's not that I don't like the rain forests, I'm crazy about them, but I think all these rock stars and Prince Charles and assorted socialites who go tearing off on fact-finding missions to Brazil are being nauseatingly trendy and don't give a damn whether the rain forests live or die, they just want their pictures taken with a darling South American Indian in a funny outfit. It makes me sick when they go all self-righteous and smug and better-than-everyone-else because they are so environmentally enlightened.

Could they stop it, please? Could they just admit they're craven little bandwagon-jumpers who've never had a single noble thought in their entire puny, horrible, meaningless little lives?

And if they won't, can we just shoot them?

A Friend of Truth

Dear Friend:

You must be the life of the party at charity balls.

So what if some of these people are assholes? So what if their motivation is selfish and stupid? So what if all they want is their names in the columns or to get invited to groovy parties? What does the rain forest care? Their money is as good as anybody else's.

People are only people, which means that 90 percent or so of their being is dedicated to self-interest. It's wonderful that the rain forest is the hottest thing of the moment—or would you prefer that making a killing in the stock market were still the thing to do? You seem to think you're the only person in the world with purity of purpose.

Go and have a nap.

Problem Lady

Dear Problem Lady:

Nightclubs! They suck.

Although I doubt it, there might actually be some interesting types going to these places, but everybody is just forced to stand and stare. They can't possibly talk, because they're blasted against the wall by the latest "house" crap. House music sucks. Fucking Vanilla Ice can blow me.

Is there anywhere to go in this town where you can meet people and have witty, or any, conversation? What would Voltaire say if he walked into one of these places? Would he ask, "Is that John Lurie?" Would he try to pick up a babe in a crushed velvet caftan?

Can you imagine Dorothy Parker in, say, Caesar's? Someone would ask her to use horticulture in a sentence but 3rd Bass would be throbbing so loud she'd just yell, "Seven-fifty for a Coke? Are they fucking nuts?"

It's true that Oscar Wilde, Mr. Perversity, would probably love night-clubs, what with all those beautiful nineteen-year-old boys in spangled hot pants hanging from every chandelier.

But listen, things are bad when I start yearning for, oh, I don't know, Studio 54 in its heyday. At least there you could look at Liza making a fool of herself on the dance floor and have engrossing conversations in the ladies' room about who might be having sex in the third stall to the left.

I'm tired of looking at pretty but inane young people saying pretty, inane things to each other in horrible boring stupid places where nothing whatsoever is going on.

Isn't there anyplace for me to go?

Chris

Dear Chris:

Nightclubs have had the same pattern of decline as rock music and lofts in Soho.

Rock music, in the sixties when it was good, was made by and for people whose brains were mangled by creativity, sex, drugs, and an over-whelming desire to have a good time. The music we hear today on "classic rock" stations was being played on obscure "underground" stations by insane hippies. Then it caught on big, people decided they could make money from it, and everything slowly but surely eroded. Now rock is controlled by horrible slimeball businessmen and large corporations and it's all boiled down to Michael Bolton.

Soho lofts used to be cheap and inhabited by starving artists. Then boring rich people, mainly dentists, decided they needed the cachet of hipness and decided to move into Soho and rub shoulders with grooviness. Next thing you know, prices were driven sky-high and Soho is a welter of shops clogged by tour buses full of middle-aged perfumed couples from Connecticut in matching fur coats looking for a cunning place to brunch. The artists have been evicted, the artists have run for their lives.

At one time nightclubs were bastions of strangeness run by insane but creative men like Steve Mass and Mickey Ruskin. A certain class of wit-infested maniacs were the principal patrons.

But unfortunately for those who liked nightclubs for the subversive thrill of decadent conversation and relaxed high jinks, nightclubs have caught on big with the college crowd—unformed youth on an allowance who will put up with anything—and with Eurotrash. They arrive in droves from all over the planet. And sleazoid businessmen with bad toupees and no penchant for fun have noticed, have taken over. Promoters are paid lots of money to give "parties" for "celebrities" who often don't even turn up. Nightclubs are now simply a business, places for tourists who don't mind being reamed.

Plus there's no sex, no drugs, so what's the point?

Stop whining and start inviting people over. It's not the same, there's no unpredictability, but it'll have to do until something better comes along.

Problem Lady

Shopping

What's a Crone to Wear?

I don't know if I'm going insane (don't answer that), but I'm walking down Melrose Avenue the other day (yes, I'm in Los Angeles, so what? I'm not having a good time or anything) and I'm popping into one store after another, looking for a long skirt, and it's like searching for the Grail.

First of all, all the clothes in the shops are heavy wool or maybe velvet. They think there's something called "winter" out here, although the Santa Ana is blowing and it's a hot, arid ninety degrees and the end of October. Even in mid-January you maybe have to wear a heavy sweater at night, but they don't care, they're going to shove wool down our throats until we gag and choke and die.

But the other thing, and this is the main thing, is that I'm looking at clothes for teenagers. And the more I look at these butt-skimming, crushed velvet sausage casings they call dresses, at the distressed leather motorcycle jackets, at the spangled T-shirts with rock stars' faces emblazoned across the chest, at the shiny spandex bicycle shorts, at the sequined bras decorated with plastic fruit, the more alienated I feel.

I can't wear these clothes. Twenty years ago I could wear these clothes because I was a teenager. Twenty years ago I wore Betsey Johnson dresses covered with giant cherries, I wore silver lamé mini-dresses with big bat-wing sleeves, I wore leather hats covered with studs. But twenty years ago I also carried a water pistol in my pocket, which I thought was hilarious, because I was a teenager. Now I am old, and I don't want to look like that. I don't want to worry about my skirt riding way up and exposing actual underwear. It's not a case of feeling wistful, these clothes are just uninteresting when you're my age.

But not as boring as the clothes in department stores, where people send me when I complain. In these hideous emporiums I see row after row of A-line skirts, silk-flowered dresses, sensible jersey separates, blouses with appliquéd flowers on them. I'm sorry, but put any of these things on my body and I'll have to go straight into a home. These are clothes worn by people who don't care about clothes, a concept I'm not quite sure I understand.

Okay, so then there's the obvious, the designer shops. Where, let's face it, it's getting more and more like you have to mortgage your house to buy a blouse. Maybe I'm insane (all right! I am!) but if I saw something that made me swoon with desire, if I saw some item of clothing that was wittily conceived, brilliantly cut, and managed to make me look ten pounds thinner, I would take out a bank loan and buy it without blinking. I used to feel this way about clothes by Romeo Gigli, by Martine Sitbon, by Sybilla, by Moschino, by Gaultier.

But Martine Sitbon has succumbed to the sixties. Sybilla, although innovative and intelligent, has forgotten that people have actual bodies, Moschino is making untranslatable jokes, Gaultier is just being goofy.

And everyone else is just doing long fitted jackets and tight skirts. Everyone. It's become the uniform of the nineties. We're now wearing our version of men's suits. I don't want to.

I wish people who design and manufacture clothes would realize that there was something called the baby boom. That right now there are more women my age than any other age. Before we came along, when women reached forty or so they became invisible. Nobody cared about them, nobody looked at them, so they slid into being boring matrons or dotty eccentrics. Only the young wore interesting clothes.

But we're not like that anymore. We've rejected those depressing role models, and we're still running around trying to have adventures. We're constantly reinventing ourselves. And we could use a few outfits.

The Goddess Regime

10 a.m. Wake up. Realize book tour is sixteen days away (and counting). Go back to sleep.

10:45 a.m. Wake up. Visions of oozing, buttery croissants and viscous honey-laced tea dance in my brain. Go to bathroom, take off clothes, get on scale. Get off scale, take off rings and watch, get on scale. Jump up and down on scale in frustration.

11 a.m. Stumble into kitchen, boil water. Pour boiling water into cup, squeeze into it one lemon. Drink and shudder. Take magnesium, chlorophyll, acidophilus, synthroid, multivitamin. Mix fiber into pear juice cut with water. Try to drink it and choke. Eat four rice cakes.

11:25 a.m. Lie on sofa, pining for chocolate.

12 p.m. Pretend to write column.

2:12 p.m. Walk very slowly up stairs to weight-lifting gym, arrive exhausted to the smell of sweaty rubber and men screaming in pain. Go to locker room, change, try to remember numbers of combination lock, look at other girl's thighs, become inconsolable.

2:30 p.m. Pedaling on stationary bicycle, watch man lift two hundred pounds and grunt. Consider having sex with this man. Adjust tension on bike. Sweat rolling down nose. Heart thinking of bursting.

2:32 p.m. Figure it must be twenty minutes by now, look at clock. Grow suicidal. Try to divert attention from clock by watching girl in a modified G-string apply lipstick while doing leg curls.

2:45 p.m. Make bargain: Stay on bicycle another five minutes and have apple as reward. Get off bike.

2:46 p.m. Sit-ups. Think about sex.

2:55 p.m. Leg lifts. Think about margaritas.

3 p.m. Hamstring stretches. Think about ex-boyfriend.

3:05 p.m. Work on lats. Think about world peace.

3:11 p.m. Have small tussle with man over chest machine. His biceps look like cantaloupes. My biceps look like sunflower seeds.

3:17 p.m. Lift twenty-five-pound barbell thirty times. Grow dizzy and strange.

3:26 p.m. Can't find triceps. Look everywhere.

3:45 p.m. Lunch: calcium, kelp, chlorophyll, mineral water, and a banana.

4 p.m. Son lying on floor watching MTV, doing homework and eating French bread pizza, pretzels, ice cream, and Mint Milanos.

4:02 p.m. Make surprise grab at Milanos, run from room clasping cookies. Son tackles me in hallway, wrests Milanos from my enervated grasp. "I'm your mother!" I yell. "Show some respect!" "Shut up, fatty," he says.

4:05 p.m. Go to room, take off clothes, look in mirror. "I am not fat!" I yell to son. Decide to lie down. Read Tolstoy.

4:50 p.m. Practice special exercises taught me by a famous teacher of lumps who have to go on talk shows. Sit up, lean forward, breathe with a silent hiss, compress abdominal muscles, and convince myself that I have just won the Nobel Prize for Literature. Then chant, "I'm glad I'm here, I'm glad you're here, I care about you, I know that I know" at breakneck speed just like I was told to. Feel like the biggest moron on earth. Quickly read more Tolstoy.

5:30 p.m. Go to nutritionist. "Definite candida implications," she says. "No bread, no mushrooms, no sugar, no vinegar, no honey, no alcohol, no milk or cheese." "Yes, I know all that," I say. "But oh please, please, please, please, can I have raisins?" "No," she says and gives me valerian root and tryptophan for my jangled nerves, reminds me to drink water.

6:15 p.m. Go to Alexander Technique class, do special stretches for spine realignment. While lifting pelvis into air, I confess to teacher that I have been lifting weights. She throws rubber balls at me. "Where have I failed you?" she cries.

7:30 p.m. Dinner with the gang. They're eating pasta with cream sauce and drinking martinis. I'm eating broiled fish, steamed vegetables, and brown rice and drinking chamomile tea. Oh life, where is thy sting?

9:15 p.m. Lew orders "chocolate pâté." Waitress brings five forks. I stealthily inch fork near pâté plate. The prongs have scooped up a dollop of whipped cream and are now imbedded in the firm chocolate. No one notices. I quietly, carefully, inch the laden fork to my mouth, open wide, and freeze. I can't do it. The fork clatters to the floor as I jump to my feet. "That's it!" I cry. "I have become a shredded-carrot person! This is the ultimate humiliation!" "Quick," says sympathetic Mary, "one sip of wine for medicinal purposes." I sip. Twice. Subside in bliss.

Full-contact Christmas Shopping

Where do they come from? They arrive in herds the Friday after Thanksgiving, their only purpose to make our lives a living nightmare. They inhabit every single cab. They angle their cars into all parking spaces. They buy the last movie tickets seconds before we arrive at the theater. They stand aimlessly on the sidewalk, stamping their feet and blowing on their hands, occasionally darting out a foot to trip a wandering passerby. They buy the last *New York Times,* clean their nails at the cash machine, pay the cashier in pennies at the supermarket, bring all traffic to a snarling standstill.

And then on January 2 they all go away again. The entire city breathes this enormous sigh of relief and then we all run out to the street, stick out our hands, and empty cabs appear. The magic is back.

The weird part is, these people don't look like out-of-towners. They don't have Jersey haircuts or funny accents, they don't consult oddly colored maps or wear pastel plaids like the invaders who come every August. They look just like us, surly and demented, but they're not us, because they disappear.

The only scientific explanation is that every year at Christmastime an alternative universe collides with ours and suddenly we are double. I know this is true because yesterday I met myself coming out of Barneys. I had a scarf on, she didn't. This put me in a bad mood, the perfect mood in which to pursue my favorite hobby:

Passive-Aggressive Gift Giving

The object is simple: to make people want to kill themselves but not know why. (N.B. Only do this to people you despise but must buy gifts for, like your immediate family.)

Say, for example, it's your cousin Laurel who lives in Dallas. She has big hair and wears little suits to her microchip marketing job. Pearl earrings, briefcase. Forty and smugly married. She's desperate to be chic the way people in Dallas always are. So what you do is buy her incredibly chic perfume which has a patchouli base. I suggest Paloma.

Laurel will splash herself liberally ("Lookit, hon, isn't the bottle just precious!"), and then she will go insane. The patchouli will work its way into her reptilian brain, dredging forth half-formed memories of her secret past when she was just another drug-soaked hippie with nasty habits. It will work just like Proust's madeleines. She'll shiver and think she's having acid flashbacks. She'll fight a searing urge for a joint. She'll have total recall of the lyrics to "Inna-Gadda-Da-Vida." Her life will be ruined and she won't know why.

Or you can buy your insufferable aunt Susan a lovely horizontally striped skirt and a box of chocolates.

Uncle Bruce, Mr. Glad-hand waitress-pincher, deserves Miles Davis's *Kind of Blue,* which will give him nightmares.

Give your mother *Helter Skelter.* Give your father *The Prophet.* Give your sister a well-framed picture of yourself. Give your brother bikini underwear.

It is true that this is evil, but not as evil as what will happen if you keep your anger bottled and seething within. You're already on the edge of homicidal mania, what with all these aliens—one with your face—running around the city. You don't want to open fire on the assorted patronage of Ray's Pizza, you want to buy your analyst a book by Leo Buscaglia.

Now you have to buy your friends presents. Which means you must brave steamy department stores with Alvin and the Chipmunks singing carols on the sound system and rampant pyramids of hideously depressing gift ideas. There's only one way to go about this.

The Pain-free Shopping Method

Buy a present for you, then a present for a friend. Then another present for you. Then a present for a friend. Then two presents for you. Then a present for a friend. Then go home, get into bed, and pull up the covers. Stay there for two days.

By this time it's probably December 23 and you've lost the will to live. Partially because it's almost Christmas and you still have twenty-three presents to buy, but also because you still don't have anything to do on New Year's Eve.

Remind yourself that nobody in this city has found a taxicab on New Year's Eve since a guy named Lenny managed it in 1953, and even then the cab was filled with the previous passenger's vomit. Repeat after me: Just stay home.

Fashion in Crisis

Hello, springtime!

Girls! Women! It's time to gather up all those bulky, drab winter clothes—those frayed brown turtlenecks covered with pills, those drooping-hemmed blanket-thick skirts, those down vests and ear-muffs—make a huge pile in your living room, and set fire to it! Clear the decks for your new, beautiful Spring clothes!

Those luscious Pucci-inspired (or even really Pucci!) prints! Those fabulous A-line, swingy, trapezy, sleeveless little dresses! Those multihued stretch pants and miniskirts, those wild, wild leggings! Time to march down to your nearest Barneys or If and grab a handful of those Christian Lacroix or faux Lacroix confections, those shrieking pink and orange and puce leggy dresses with swirls or squares or polka dots or whatever! Peplums! The sixties are back with a vengeance and isn't it madly thrilling?

Ha ha ho ho hee hee hee.

Boy they really have it wrong this time. This is much, much worse than the great maxiskirt fiasco of 1970.

I mean, have all fashion designers lost their minds or what? Have you seen the stuff in the shops? Who wants to wear that trash? Who's going to march into Bergdorf's and say, "Gimme that little powder blue and magenta bolero jacket with that lovely kelly-green skirt for twenty-four hundred dollars"?

It's bad enough that they seem to have had some secret summit conference where they all took acid and sat around and decided, "The sixties! That's what they all want! We'll make a killing!" That's muddy-headed and stupid and boring enough. But what's even worse is that we're not seeing racks and racks of the clothing that young people wore in the sixties. We're seeing racks and racks of what young people's *mothers* wore in the sixties.

I was there! I know! Nobody was wearing Pucci or those hideous little crisp dresses! We were wearing nightgowns that we cut off just below the crotch with fishnet stockings! We were wearing little gray knit Paraphernalia dresses sprinkled with purple bows! We were wearing sleazy bat-winged satin dresses with glass buttons! We were wearing black witch's shoes with heels going the wrong way, goddammit!

Okay, wait a minute. I have to calm down.

I can't calm down! It's *exactly* the opposite now of the way it was then! Then, we just wanted to be weird and goofy and creative. Then, we were using clothes to illustrate a new consciousness—an antiestablishment, antiwar, prolove, pro-sex-with-anyone-and-everyone-we-could-fit-into-our-beds kind of consciousness. A consciousness of infinite possibilities, a consciousness of exhilarated optimism. We didn't care about money as status, we were the counterculture. We hated the government, we hated authority, we hated conventionalism.

Ha ha hee hee.

So what kind of sick, *demented* joke is it that has us now walking down the street, seeing those horrible little American flags waving everywhere? Walking down the street seeing Silence = Death posters, walking down the street and hearing of yet another AIDS death, and then, needing to buy a new outfit, needing to cheer ourselves up, walking into a store and seeing hideous retreads of a time when sex was free and flags were for burning? What do they think those clothes are doing besides *underlining* our tragedies?

I blame these fashion designers, how could they be so stupid? I know, I know, times are tough and scary, nobody's buying anything, and when nobody buys the people who produce run scared, refuse to take risks. They run home and curl themselves up into little balls of fear and their minds go blank. And fashion designers are especially hard hit—their ranks have been horribly decimated by disease, and conspicuous consumption is dead. Nobody but a moron wants to parade around in a jacket that blares its stupefying price.

But come on, the sixties is no solution! Those clothes are going to rot on those racks! We don't want them! Only the most slavish and silly of fashion clones would be caught dead in the stuff!

And meanwhile, the rest of us have nothing to wear except the clothes we wore last year and we don't want to wear them because even last year at this time we were still under the spell of the eighties, we were still walking around in our Gaultiers and our Armanis that we bought at Century 21 or Dollar Bills, we were still using clothes to proclaim our social superiority.

We know better now. World events have changed us. But they haven't changed us so much that we crave white go-go boots, okay?

Dear Problem Lady:

It's that dreadful season. That blood-chilling, mind-numbing, heart-stopping, stomach-curdling time of year. The time when droves of healthy, happy, normal, law-abiding, and sober women suddenly are compelled to leap from very high windows and splatter themselves on the sidewalk.

Bathing suit season.

It's bad enough having to appear in these monstrous jokes of fabric. Bad enough to pretend to sashay casually down the beach pretending not to be about to burst into tears at the thought of hundreds of strangers looking at your naked thighs, hundreds of strangers wanting to throw up when they see those stomach rolls, those drooping knees.

But much, much worse is when you need a new one. When you're imprisoned in the dressing room of a department store with one dozen hideously mocking bits of frill that look perfectly friendly on the hanger but the minute you try them on reveal themselves as the instruments of torture they are.

I'm about to go to Macy's. My vision's blurry and I think I'm going to throw up. Would it be better to just stay indoors for the entire summer?
A Friend

Dear Friend:

First of all, you know those strangers on the beach? They're not looking at you, they don't care whether you live or die. They're just hoping you don't notice that their butts are more bovine than any cow's. At least the women are. The men, even the pear-shaped ones, all think they, themselves, look lovely. And they're in such a state of erotic overstimulation that they can't even focus on body blemishes, they just want to fuck whatever they see.

Do not go to Macy's. Go nowhere where there is the kind of unnatural overhead lighting that would make Linda Evangelista's thighs look like a hippo's. Go to little shops where there is sunlight and salespeople with no attitude.

And think creatively. I know a woman who wears thigh-hiding bicycle shorts and a matching halter top. Made of leopard print fabric, so people think she's sexy.

Problem Lady

Dear Problem Lady:

An English fashion designer told me to wear high heels with jeans. Should I listen?

Cindy

Dear Cindy:

No.

Problem Lady

Dear Problem Lady:

Please tell me why lingerie saleswomen are the scum of the earth.

I went into this place on Greenwich Avenue the other day. There was a woman behind the counter. "Do you have control top . . ." I said, and already she was shaking her head.

"We don't carry control top," she minced.

"Opaque pantyhose?" I continued.

"Absolutely none," she said.

"Well excuse me for being so tacky," I said.

"It's not that I'm rude," she opined, "it's just that we feel you can buy your control top at a drugstore."

And then you know that special look that certain people, notably New

Yorkers with a social-climbing bent, like to give people? That sarcastic "you pathetic fool I'm only humoring you" gaze? She gave me one.

I left the shop feeling not only like a moron, but like a really fat moron for wanting opaque control top. Which one cannot buy at a drugstore.

Is it just me?

Sincerely,
Madeleine X

Dear Madeleine:

It is not just you. It is just them.

You must stop to ask yourself, "What kind of woman would work amongst G-strings all day?" I did, and realized that anybody might, but that prolonged exposure to crinolines, push-up bras, and seamed stockings will work on a specific part of a girl's brain, that part that hates other women and wants all men to herself.

Before she knows it, this usually small and hidden area of the cortex has become cancerous, spreads, and voilà! She's a competitive shrew.

Then you walk into the shop and she wants you dead.

Problem Lady

Battle of the Sexes

What's a Guy to Do?

I'm still trying to figure out why men are in such trouble.

Oh, come on, you know you are. You're bewildered, insecure, and terribly nervous. You're confused not only about how to act with women, but how to relate to the entire world. You've been buffeted by constant social and sexual conflicts and have lost control of all inner equilibrium.

I see you on talk shows attempting to explain yourself to audiences of sneering women. I see you pouring into twelve-step meetings, where you try to cry in front of people. But worst of all, I'm starting to see you at bookstores furtively buying self-help books.

The buying of a self-help book is the most desperate of all human acts. It means you've lost your mind completely: You've entrusted your mental health to a self-aggrandizing twit with a psychology degree and a yen for a yacht. It means you're having a major identity crisis.

Women did this a while ago, when our sex was having an identity crisis that lasted for oh, a decade. We didn't know who we were supposed to be, so we mainlined annoying tomes like *Women Who*

Love Too Much. But then along came Anita Hill. She was the ignition that switched on everywoman's brain. Before Anita, we were all whining, "What's wrong with me? Where can I find a book to fix me?" After Anita, we all decided, "Wait a minute! It isn't me after all! Women are *still* being fucked over in our society!"

We're feeling much better now, thank you.

But men are feeling worse. You've been through a lot of identity-battering in the last twenty years:

First, you had to unlearn everything you were ever taught about women when feminism came along. You thought that you were supposed to grow up, get married, and immediately become the captain of the ship, the breadwinner. All that responsibility was scary, but a man had to do what a man had to do.

Then you were told that that was all wrong and how dare you? It was time to give up half your power to women or else.

Some of you became recalcitrant pigs, but many of you tried. You tried to be sensitive, you tried to learn the new language of women, you tried to gently abdicate your heavy mantle of responsibility, you tried to treat women as equal.

Then you were told that that was all wrong and how come you were all such wimps? What woman wanted a man she could walk all over?

So then you all bought motorcycle jackets and grew little pony-tails and sported a three-day growth of beard and tried to be neo-tough. The message was "No broad better push me around, and if she does, well, I'll . . . I'll . . . be sensitive and caring."

That didn't work, because women were going through their aforementioned crisis around then and nothing you did pleased us. Nothing.

Then along came Robert Bly and the masculinist movement and

suddenly many of you found yourself spending nights in the woods, sweating and beating drums. Or at least reading about it.

But that felt just too goofy, and you had bigger problems. The economy plunged disastrously and many people lost jobs. Maybe not you. But maybe you soon. Plus women were charging you with sexual harassment and date rape. Maybe not you. But maybe you soon.

At this point in history, does it feel like you can't do anything right?

It's time to realize that there's nothing wrong with you. Well, there's plenty wrong with *some* of you. Men who abuse women, men who take the anger in their souls out on women, men who think of women as sex objects to be used and discarded should not even be allowed to be called men. But most of you are well-meaning but hopelessly befuddled.

So you're buying self-help books, you're blaming yourselves for your own unhappiness, you think you have some fatal flaw that reading some book will put right.

But it's not you. Society is fucking you over. Society has taken away all possible role models.

The last role model you had was "breadwinner, captain of the family." You could go ahead and become that, or you could become some kind of James Dean/Jack Nicholson guy and rebel against everything and run away. Either choice gave you a built-in structure in your attitudes toward women: You were either totally responsible or totally irresponsible. Either choice was sanctioned by society.

Now these choices have been systematically destroyed and replaced with nothing. There's nothing you're supposed to be, there's nothing to rebel against being.

You're working in a void, without identity, and the only messages you receive are negative: Don't be a pig, don't be a wimp.

Many of you have taken refuge in careers, defining yourselves solely by your jobs. This doesn't work anymore either. You're having heart attacks, you're getting fired.

Okay, I'm not a man. But I have been through a period of my life where it was either reinvent yourself or kill yourself. And I say it's time for a masculine revolution.

This means you've got to stop listening to anybody. Stop listening to a society which tells you you're powerful when in fact a couple of rich guys control everything. Stop listening to beer commercials which instruct you to be a moron. Stop listening to women who don't know what the hell they want but want you to give it to them anyway. Follow your best instincts. Figure out what's important to you.

Maybe you could reinvent the concept of fatherhood. Everybody seems to be decrying the lack of fathers, nobody seems to know what fathers are supposed to do. Maybe you can drop that heavy cloak of "manliness" that keeps you acting silent and strong when you want to be gossipy and playful.

Oh, don't listen to me, either. Just make it up as you go along. Just stop moping before we all go insane.

The Female Animal

Men! Want to know if a woman is interested in you? Here is the most important rule:

All you really need to know you learned in high school.

Even if you're eighty-four, it always is and always will be high school. It's true that people grow older, more sophisticated, but nobody ever matures past age eighteen. The same feelings persist. The way we acted then is the way we act now, even though our braces no longer lock when we kiss.

Okay, so what does a teenaged girl do when she's crazy for a guy? She ignores him, and talks about him incessantly to her friends. She only looks at him when she's positive he's not looking at her. She fidgets, she stammers, she's tongue-tied and stumbles over nothing when he's around. She draws curly hearts with his initials in them on her desk. She memorizes his phone number, calls him frequently, always hangs up when he answers.

She acts as if she couldn't care whether he lived or died, yet she's always around. Somehow she's wandering mindlessly through the gym during basketball practice. She's suddenly secretary of the debating club. She's tooling her bike, no hands, down his street. She's dropped her books all over his corner.

We're still the same. Ever wonder why Paige in accounting always needs a drink of water when you do? Why every night she's in the same elevator when you go home? Paige wants you.

So why won't Paige flirt with you? She can't. A woman can start out all giggly and flirty, but at some point consciousness sets in: "Oh my God, I like this guy. I want to sleep with this guy. This could be the guy for me."

And crowding the heels of consciousness is *self*-consciousness. "My God, what if this guy knows I like him? He'd just laugh and laugh. He must have noticed that I'm a dork and that this dress I'm wearing is just hideous. I can't smile. If I smile he'll see my teeth. I probably have spinach in my goddamned horrible ugly teeth. I know I have two half-moons of mascara under my eyes. I have to go to the bathroom, right now."

That's why the girl you thought you were doing great with runs away. And won't come back. She'll go to the other side of the room and not look at you at all, and you're supposed to know she wants you to come after her.

Unfortunately, this is also the way a woman acts when she really isn't interested. So you're screwed. The only way to get around this other-side-of-the-room business is to go *halfway* across the room, as if you're on your way over but didn't quite make it. This will drive her insane and she'll have to come to you.

Now is the best time to ask her to dinner. Don't just ask for her phone number.

If you ask for her phone number she will immediately and automatically envision herself sitting day after day on her sofa, bleary-eyed and twitching, waiting for you to call. And right then and there, she will hate you; she will never want to see you again.

All of us, even fourteen-year-olds, have wasted a large percentage of our lives waiting by the phone. (I myself, by recent calculation, have spent four years, three months, and twelve days biting my nails and staring. Now instead, I ask the guy for *his* number, which doesn't help at all, since it takes me approximately five hours to work up my nerve to call, by which time it's invariably two a.m.)

So ask her to dinner. If she accepts, she's interested.

And this is major: If, when you go out to dinner, she doesn't look really dressed up or anything but somehow she looks *thinner,* she's madly in love with you.

When women are excited about a date, they go immediately on a diet, because all women know they are hideously obese. Even if the diet doesn't work, even if she only loses four ounces, she will relentlessly try on everything in her wardrobe to find the outfit that turns her most strandlike. Then she'll go shopping and repeat the process. But she won't get all gussied up because she thinks that if she did you'd know she cares and you'd drop her flat.

If she touches you a lot for no reason, she's interested. If you move closer to her and she doesn't move away, she's interested. If every time you look at her she quickly looks away, she's interested. If you see her grocery shopping in your neighborhood, she's interested.

If she sleeps with you on the first date she's foolish, but interested. If she doesn't sleep with you after the fifth date she's either actually still in high school, born again, or not interested, no matter what she says.

And that brings me to the painful part. Sometimes women really aren't interested. And many guys, caught up with their own enthusiasm, refuse to notice. So they pursue and persist, and then they get furious and use the word "bitch" too often in a sentence.

Sometimes women are not as sensitive as they should be. Sometimes they're too sensitive, they make the mistake of leading you on so they won't disappoint you.

Please, for your own mental health, look for these early warning signs:

1. If she flirts with you incessantly and seems supremely self-confident but is never available for dates, leave her alone, she's only kidding.

2. If you both leave somewhere at the same time and she says "See ya!," waves, and disappears, you bore her.

3. If you ask her out twice and she can't go, don't ask her again.

4. If she says she's going to call you and you wait and wait, join the club.

Time: Killer or Joker?

My childhood is like an acid flashback. Vague faces swim toward me when I try to remember grade school, junior high or high school. I had a best friend Amy but I only remember thick green leaves, her father's pipe in a white room, Amy on the swing with her braids flying backward. I had a friend named Polly Roach who drew horses incessantly. I was madly in love in the fifth and sixth grades with Jerry Bass, just like everyone else. I wrote his name over and over in my book. There was a boy named Ronnie Kessler, I think he was in love with me, I should have married him. There was Libby, who was boy-crazy . . .

But I am a grown-up now, I have reinvented myself. I live in New York, far from the Main Line. People who know me now don't know I was stupid and unpopular. I've escaped. So when my friend Sarah, who I met when we were four and still know and love, said she was going to the high school reunion, I said I'd go. It would be so funny.

We were early. Also early were two women named Karen and Cindy, whom I'd never seen before. Karen showed me her junior high yearbook. There was my picture, across which I had written, "Karen,

It was a great time! Hope we see each other again! Love, Cyndy." Sarah found this hilarious.

Soon we were enmeshed in predinner cocktails and a blonde came up. "I thought of you yesterday," she said.

"Why, Gibble?" I asked. I hadn't thought of her yesterday. But now it was as if I'd seen her yesterday in study hall.

"Because I saw Reggie Jackson on TV," she said. She was obliquely alluding to the old scandal. I got very nervous and went and chomped on a carrot stick. Then I saw Polly Roach across the room and started choking.

"But you're blonde!" I said to Polly after she used the Heimlich maneuver. She had exactly the same face.

"I don't know how it happened," Polly said. Then Debbie Lieberman wafted by and Polly went quiet. Only minutes ago I wouldn't have recognized the name. But now I pictured little Debbie Lieberman being mean to little Polly Roach because Polly didn't chase boys or try to be popular or anything, Polly just drew horses and sang in the choir and was nice to everyone.

"Hi, Cyndy," said a very pretty girl. I looked at her blankly. "Suzie Boyer," she said, "you don't remember me?"

"Oh of course I do," I said. I didn't really.

"Heartbreaker alert! Heartbreaker alert!" Sarah was running toward us and screaming. "Jerry Bass has arrived! He's still gorgeous!"

I felt a wave of fear. "I'm not talking to him," I said. "Fine," said Sarah, "I am." And she left.

"I remember you giving a book report in the eighth grade where you used the word 'Jew,' " said Suzie, "I'd never heard it before." She was beginning to look familiar.

"Oh my God, will you look at that, Nan is a redhead," I said to Polly.

Polly laughed. "Same old Cyndy," she said. Oh, no.

"Petey died of a heart attack three months ago," Nan whispered to me.

"Oh Jesus," I said, "and Major has gone insane. This is terrible."

"And Harvey's in jail," said Libby, "for rape." Libby looked the same but was serene. "I didn't get married until I was twenty-nine," she said. "It was the right thing to do."

"I remember you," said a completely unfamiliar man. "My friend was so in love with you all through junior high and high school, until you left. He wanted to go out with you so much. You're all he ever talked about."

"Who? Who?" I asked frantically, wondering if it was too late.

"I can't remember his name, but all the boys were in love with you, you were a sexpot," he said.

I think he was talking about someone else and just got the names wrong.

Jerry Bass, looking so gorgeous, walked by, smiled, and waved. I looked around, realized I was alone at the table, and blushed.

"You didn't graduate with us," accused a very short girl.

"No I didn't," I snapped. "My parents pulled me out of school because I wouldn't stop going out with Major, okay?"

"And Libby was going out with Harvey, and Nan was going out with Petey, but it was just a fad with them, and you stayed with Major for years."

"Nobody would care if you went out with a black guy these days," said Gibble, "times have changed."

But the times hadn't helped Major, now insane, or Harvey, now in jail, or Petey, now dead. It had just been too hard.

Jerry Bass, who is now a psychotherapist, walked up to me and introduced himself! "I know," I said, "I was totally in love with you." And I still am. A deep and abject love was hurtling up from my unconscious, still insanely intact. "Everybody was."

"No, really? I had no idea. Really? I wish I had known," he said with that sweet stutter I'd forgotten. "Nobody ever knows. We're all prisoners of our own childhood fears."

I walked away from him with heart aching. Sarah and I hugged everyone and said good-bye. Suzie Boyer was now vivid in my memory, I pictured her in home ec, on overnights with the Brownies. It was as if I had known her all my life.

Gay Blades

Nigel was rouging and powdering my cleavage, George was blow-drying my bangs, I was wriggling.

"Ow!"

"Stay still," said George. "Do you or do you not want to look like Christie Turlington?"

"Christ, now I've rouged your collarbone," said Nigel. "Stop fidgeting. There. You look fabulous."

"Fabulous," said George. "Stunning."

"So would either of you like to fuck me?"

"I would, but I must condition my chest hair," said George, sweeping from the room.

"Would you like to suck a large milky-white tit?" Nigel asked me.

"Please, Nige," I said.

"How about licking a pussy?"

"Please! Gross me out!"

"And that's how we feel," said Nigel.

Gender identification is a tricky thing. Should I resent Nige and

George for not paying me the ultimate compliment of their sexual desire? Should I consider them misogynists for their aversion? Or should I, as I do, love them because they're my dear friends and understand me better than a thousand straight men?

Not that there aren't gay misogynists:

What's the difference between a woman and a bowling ball?

If you had to, you could fuck a bowling ball.

Why are women like dog turds?

The older they are, the easier they are to pick up.

I heard both of these jokes from gay men about a decade ago, but I'll never forget them or stop despising the men who told them. But those are two instances in ten years, whereas every day of my life I am buffeted, no, fuck it, I am smashed in the face with heterosexual misogyny. Woman hatred explodes from my TV set, from the guys with jackhammers on my street, from waiters, from novelists. Straight men want to fuck women, and too often that makes them hate women.

So call me a fag hag if you want.

"You fag hag," says Nigel.

"There, you see!" I say, "gay men are always the ones to say it! They're always the first to put themselves down. Gay men are full of self-loathing!"

"So are women."

"That's true. Sometimes I think that self-loathing is the most humanizing of influences. We hate ourselves, therefore we have great compassion for others."

"Unless of course we hate ourselves and therefore go out and machine-gun an entire village."

"There is that. Maybe we feel bound to each other by our oppression. We are united in our helpless resentment of the oppressor, the heterosexual white male. We identify with each other's plight."

"We identify with each other's tragically futile lust for Dennis Quaid, you silly cow."

"We have the same sexual impulses, yet we're not competitive, the way women can be. It's perfect."

"Has anybody seen my champagne-bucket earrings?" George called from the bathroom.

Gay men identify with women, in camp moments they yell at each other "girlfriend!" or even "girleen!," but they are not women. In their sexual behavior, they are alarmingly male.

Prowling, predatory, easily excited into lust, willing and able to have sex with those they regard with indifference or even hold in contempt. This explains the tragic promiscuity that went on before we knew about AIDS. Imagine what it would be like if you, a straight man, were met with a lusty, eager acceptance by every woman you ogled on the street or in a bar. That's what gay life was like in the seventies.

"Well, thank you very much," said George, "as if I would ever do it with anybody else but my Nige."

"You won't, George, but you might want to. Remember that guy who came to pick me up the other night?"

"Oh, he was so dishy. So gorgeous. Those eyes!"

"That's what I mean. Men, biologically, are helplessly promiscuous. The more evolved ones can rein in their animal impulses."

"Oh shut up and let's go to the party," said Nigel, making his James Dean face in the mirror.

At the party they got wild, Nigel danced with all the girls, holding them close, grinding into them.

"Nigel, be careful, she's a flower," George cautioned.

"You're just a closet heterosexual, Nigel," I accused.

Then the hostess brought out her wigs, and all the straight men in the room, heady with drink, tried them on and flounced around. They were adorable.

"That one doesn't know it yet," said Nigel, gesturing, "but he plays on our team."

"Yes," I said, "I thought he was awfully nice."

Yes, I mean it! Gay men are nicer! You can talk to them! And not because they're willing to chat about hairdos! You can say personal, complicated things to a gay man, and he won't look at you fishily, he won't make you feel like a fool.

There is a terrible pride about straight men. An implacable rigidity. They seem to forever be holding themselves in check, as if they're denying a convoluted maelstrom of feelings and fears churning within them. As if they're afraid that even one chink in their armor will make them fall apart.

So vehemently in control, and therefore so clearly vulnerable, straight men reduce women to uncertainty and delicacy. We're afraid we'll wound you and compromise your potency. We become your nursemaids.

The best, and perversely, the most masculine of straight men are the ones who have a strong dollop of femininity in their makeup. Give me a straight man who isn't afraid to gossip, whose mouth doesn't tighten when confronted by a woman being raunchy.

Femininity makes you strong.

Aging: Fact or Fiction?

I found out tonight that a fellow I have my eye on is forty-five years old and even though I'm hardly younger I briefly thought, "Am I too old for him? He's adorable and hilarious, he'll probably want someone around twenty-four." I got this idea from another guy I had an affair with several years ago, who is now fifty, and has a new girlfriend who is twenty-two.

My birthday is coming up next week! I'm getting old! It's a little depressing!

Here's the worst thing: My sex objects are too young for me. I sit on my sofa of an evening and watch basketball, oft consumed by dizzying lust. It is just slightly possible that Pat Riley might give me a whirl, but Michael Jordan is out of my ballpark. He would probably call me ma'am and help me across the street if we ever met, I could never get him into bed unless he had some kind of kinky attraction to someone old enough to be his mother (if she got pregnant in the sixth grade).

Aging, everybody knows, is the final, irrevocable inequity between the sexes. A man in his forties wouldn't have a bit of trouble dating a girl Michael Jordan's age. Men in their forties are sexy, just reaching their prime, with interesting *lines* in their faces which make them look *rugged*. Whereas women who have *wrinkles* on their faces are considered *raddled*.

Here's what I think the problem is: makeup. You won't see Clint Eastwood wearing blusher.

Wearing makeup is asking for approval. Wearing makeup is an apology for our actual faces. Wearing makeup makes it seem as if a woman has something to hide. Wearing makeup makes a woman look older than she actually is.

Wearing makeup means "I am a sexual object of prey. Come after me." Prepubescent girls look absurd in eyeliner, because they are sending a false message. The same is true for mature women who, once they're in their forties, should have full command of their own powers, sexual or otherwise, and have no right to be offering themselves up as prey. (And now I should probably go underground, in case all those companies that place all those full-page makeup ads in fashion magazines send out hit men.)

Okay, from now on I will let my crow's-feet run free. But then there's the rest of my body.

It wants to thicken. I used to go on a diet once every three years, it took that long for my weight to creep up to unacceptable. Now every day I strap weights around my ankles and wrists and jump for half an hour on my trampoline. And I don't drink. If I drink I get puffy. Well, sometimes I drink. Sometimes I inhale a vat of margaritas because I just don't give a flying fuck, who the hell cares if I'm old and wide and sagging? If people don't like it they don't have to look at me.

But then I see Michael Jordan on TV, or walk down my street where many very young men parade by wearing tank tops. I curse the sexual urge, it makes fools of us all!

Nature makes sure that humans who can produce children look

more sexually riveting than those who cannot, a little trick to continue the species. Even an eighty-year-old man can father a child, but a woman over fifty would be hard-pressed.

But nature fucked up! Men are convulsively horny when they are seventeen! By twenty-five they start stabilizing, by sixty-five they get it up only if they pray a little.

Not so with women! We get hornier and hornier! Some days I wake up moist, and I *know* that this is going to be one of those days when I start prowling the streets in tight black clothes and high heels, lust driving me into insane and sometimes hilarious frenzies. A friend who saw me slink around a nightclub one evening phoned me the next morning: "This is the hormone police," he said, "we're getting dangerous readings from your apartment, you are quarantined until further notice."

"Perhaps a house call would be in order," I cooed.

Not that I would actually do it with him. Call it age, call it AIDS, but directly proportional to my tidal wave of sexuality is my absolute conservatism. I want to, oh I want to, but I won't go to bed with anybody. I remember too well what it all means. I am scarred, I am distrustful, I am gun-shy, I'm afraid, I'm too damned old to be madly impulsive!

At these nightclubs where I prowl, there are many children with smooth, luminous faces who look at me like I'm a schoolteacher as they fall about in each other's arms. I want to say to them, "Be careful! Get it right the first time, or at least the second. Give your innocent heart and soul to someone good for you, someone who likes you, before you get callous and twisted."

And I remember me as a teenager in a miniskirt with fishnet stockings and a purple vinyl trench coat and a floppy felt hat, with a water pistol in my pocket and a boy on each arm, living with a rock-and-roll band, careening through my youth. I remember riding on the back of a motorcycle, holding on for dear life to a boy whose body was better than Michelangelo's *David,* I swear. I remember falling in love with a series of boys with hair flapping in their eyes and skin like milk.

I remember how hilarious it was to walk in summer storms and get soaked to the skin, with my dress clinging to my body and every pore of my being filled with the joy of being a goofy girl. And going back to my first apartment with the beaded curtains. Smoking pot and panhandling in the park. Meeting my future husband on Avenue C in New York, falling immediately in love and having a baby. It was easy, I could have done it with my hands tied behind my back.

Do you know what? I have spent a full twenty years watching boys play guitars! First it was my rock-and-roll band, every one of whom was my boyfriend at one time or another. Then it was my husband, then the fellow I lived with, and of course all my girlfriends' boyfriends. Now my son! "Listen to this, Mom," he says, and I realize he's playing the overture to *Tommy,* the rock opera, and I vividly remember sitting at Roger Daltrey's feet in a nearly deserted rock club while he swung his microphone inches from my nose.

I was at a rock club the other night, very hard core, and there were all these girls in bits of clothes, all ripped and transparent and sexy. A matronly woman was standing next to me. "See those girls?" she asked. "They're me. I know what I look like on the outside, but on the inside I'm just like that."

And I thought: Not me, I've been there, I've had a good run, but enough is enough.

Although right now I'm sleeping with a twenty-seven-year-old cowboy. Maybe I'm overreacting.

Asking for Trouble

"That one, black leather vest, over there," I said.

"Don't look; he's looking at us."

Lucy swiveled discreetly. "Plaid shirt? You're not serious."

"No, no. The one with the nose."

"That's better. Yes, very nice. Very tasty. Looks like he'd beat you up if you asked him to. Even if you didn't ask."

"Trouble," I crooned across the room in the Lone Star Café in New York City, "come to Momma."

And of course he did. And of course he had three ex-wives, had done time, flaunted a serious cocaine problem, and thought that Hank Williams, Jr., was a much better singer than his daddy.

"I can't stand a man who thinks Hank Jr. can sing better than Hank," I said to Lucy. "Let's leave."

Of course I'm kidding! Of course I wouldn't pick up a man with ex-wives and prison sentences and drug addictions in a bar! What do you think I am?

Well, anyway, I wouldn't have left with him. No way would I have walked into the night with such a stranger on my arm. But it is possible that if he had better musical preferences, hadn't doused himself with after-shave, had talked to me about his existential angst, looked misunderstood, called me darlin' and told me a good joke, I might have taken his number.

Do I hear the sound of a million men slapping their foreheads and cursing? Are many of you thinking, Dames! You try to be sensitive, be good to them, give them equal rights, and what happens? They revolve right out the nearest door with a bozo with tattooed knuckles!

Not too long ago, I was watching "Love Connection," a TV show where you get to choose your dates, and there was this adorable guy on, looking for love. "I don't understand," he said something like. "I wash their cars, paint their houses, pick them up after work, take care of their kids, and women don't like me."

"Oh, you moron!" I yelled at the TV. "Why don't you just lie down on a platter and put an apple in your mouth?"

Yes, it's true: Women are perverse. We like trouble. Some of us court it like hotheaded kamikaze pilots. Others of us are content to go once a year to a Clint Eastwood movie. But we all want it. It's the curse of our existence. Several books have been written on the subject. Millions of hours of therapy have been spent. I should do a best-selling video on the subject and make a million dollars.

There are reasons.

A man who will paint your house will cook you meat loaf. A man who will cook you meat loaf will want to watch you shave your legs. A man who will want to watch you shave your legs will hold your hand and cry at sad AT&T commercials. A man who will hold your hand and cry at sad AT&T commercials will fall apart if you leave him.

We can't stand this. It makes us feel all weird and responsible and claustrophobic, as if this man who paints our house can't tell where his personality ends and ours begins. A man who paints our house is a man, we feel, who wants to merge. A man who will look at us with eager puppy-dog eyes when we are trying to get the bills paid. A door mat. Door mats are scary; they need too much. We like someone we can collide with who won't fall down; we like resistance. There is nothing as unattractive as a man collapsing at one's feet. Someone who doesn't need us is a lot less scary than someone who needs us too much.

So we'll go for a guy who gives us that crucial distance, who forgets to call, fails to buy flowers, has difficulty remembering our names. I know it's dumb.

There's more: When we fall flat on our faces for the crazed sculptor who drinks himself into a stupor whenever possible, or the lecherous tramp who wants to put a bag over our heads, what it really means is that we want to be that fellow. We want to be the self-destructive artist who goes on such a bender that three full days are lost from his memory. We want to fuck everyone we see. But women don't do this. Or maybe they do, but then they're not cool.

Difficult men are considered cool, romantic, interesting. Difficult women are considered deranged, sicko, neurotic nymphos. So we see a fellow who is trouble and we identify. All those secret subterranean urges that we deny in ourselves are manifested in this man, and we fall madly in love with him, often not even vaguely understanding that we're falling in love with an aspect of ourselves that we've denied, hidden, blocked, felt terribly ashamed of, ignored. Before I was a writer, I had a husband who was a painter but a passive guy. He could hardly tie his own shoelaces. So I took over. I got his paintings off the floor and into frames. I sent him to art galleries. I made him go after dealers and buyers. I pushed that poor fellow mercilessly. Meanwhile, when I wasn't helping my spouse, I was languishing in bed, eating cookies and watching soap operas. I had no life of my own. I was living through my alleged better half. I couldn't figure out why I was depressed.

Then the penny dropped and I ended my marriage and started working. My ex-husband is still confused. I tell him women often submerge the stronger, more difficult, selfish, interesting parts of their personalities and live through others. He still doesn't understand why baking cakes isn't enough.

I have seen healthy women's eyes go limpid and their voices become husky with lust when bad boys are mentioned. If you don't have real excitement in your life, you'll go for it in bed.

Here's my proposed scenario for you good, sensitive, understanding guys: Say you've got a crush on an adorable girl named Gladys, but Gladys is mad for some guy who crushes beer cans on his forehead. Here's what you do. Say, "Gladys, haven't you always wanted to play the saxophone?"

"So?" she'll ask.

"Quit your accounting job, Gladys; you know you hate it. Get the goddamned saxophone out of mothballs and go for it. Start hanging around all night in smoky jazz clubs, practicing licks."

"My hero," Gladys will say to you.

Chasing Children

In the Irish night the moon looked smudged and insecure through the microscopic mist droplets. My face and raincoat were soaked. I had a huge scarf tied around my head, looking like my own Jewish grandmother as I stood at the edge of the lake in a quiet valley surrounded by the hulking mountains of Connemara. I heard a dog bark from a farmhouse a mile away. The eighteen-year-old boy put his arm around my waist. "Kiss me," he said.

I don't like the way things have shaped up with this Woody Allen thing. When the news first came out, I didn't want to be one of the knee-jerk feminists booing during *Husbands and Wives*. I was prepared to be magnanimous, prepared not to exactly forgive but to feel compassion for the self-destructive behavior of our beloved tortured genius. I wanted everyone to pity the man, not ostracize him.

What I wasn't prepared for was the elasticity of our collective unconscious. Somehow society has stretched itself to absorb Woody's peccadilloes. Somehow everybody thinks it's okay that he's sleeping with his ex-girlfriend's daughter. In fact it's more than okay, Woody has made old men with young girls downright *trendy*.

Jesus. If Mia had done the same thing she would have been everyone's object of ridicule. People regard older women who have young lovers as both predatory and pathetic. Whereas geriatric men with college girls are *studs*. Men get every fucking break.

Just before I went to Ireland I went with my comedian friend to a Malibu party. There was this guy there, I'm not mentioning names but he was a famous activist in the sixties and then became a chic lefty politician. Dogs and children romped in the waves as body-building caterers served turkey-burgers. Mr. Activist picked up the phone and dialed. "Could you please bring the dog over now," he said and paused. "I know you're sick, but I'd really like you to bring the dog over now, please."

Moments later a pretty young girl with runny eyes and a red nose arrived with a panting yellow Lab. "You're not mad at me, are you?" she asked the activist.

"Goddammit," I said to my comedian, "you know why men like younger women?"

"Because of their petal-soft flesh and perky breasts?" he asked.

"A young woman is the perfect status symbol for men to show off to their friends, plus they think it will be easier to boss a young girl around. They're right. Grown women as a rule don't take as much shit from men as young girls do."

"Although some guys want total control," the comedian said, "other guys want a woman to have adventures with and tell everything to and fall down laughing with."

"That makes me feel better," I said grudgingly.

"Of course if she's a twenty-two-year-old leggy supermodel, so much the better," he added.

*   *   *

Not that I blame men. Okay I do, but only because I am a bad sport. It's biology's fault. Nature is not a feminist. If nature were a feminist women would have no biological clock and no menopause. Instead of being born with all the eggs we'll ever have, women would produce new eggs until we were eighty, giving birth would be a breeze, and there would be no such thing as a stretch mark. Men would run out of sperm when they were fifty whereupon everyone would approve as we dumped our worn-out, flabby husbands and scooped up young dudes and started a whole new life, a whole new family.

But nature doesn't care about women, nature only cares about the perpetuation of the species. Nature is a bitch.

On the way to Ireland I stopped in London to visit Louisa. We lay on the floor of her flat stuffing ourselves with cream cakes and discussing why men chase babies. I told her my theories of status, power.

"I don't think it's that," Louisa said. "I think men fear aging, which means they fear death, which means if they find a young popsie without crow's-feet they think they'll live forever."

"But it doesn't work that way at all," I said. "When I was with the Kiwi, who was eleven years younger, I felt old and *silly*. If anything, being with him underlined my fears of aging, my fears of death."

"Which," said Louisa, "simply proves you are not a man."

In Ireland I looked up my friend Jenny. Jenny had had a fairy-tale romance with her boss, fifteen years older. He swept her off her feet. She was the most ecstatic bride, going from a low-paid clerk to Lady of the Manor with a glamorous, dashing husband. We arranged to meet in a pub.

Jenny arrived, thin as a stick. "I'm leaving him," she said, puffing greedily on a cigarette. "All he wants to do is hang around with his old friends and play bridge. He never wants to go out dancing or anything, and it's gross when he wants to have sex. He's got so many love handles he needs a bookmark to find his shorts.

"If he'd only do things on the spur of the moment, just once in a while, I could take it. But he's so careful, so bossy, so dull! I'm young. I need fun! I need excitement! In twenty years he'll be dead and I won't be pretty anymore!"

"And here everyone thought you were Cinderella," I said.

Jenny stubbed out her cigarette. "If there's one thing I've learned, it's that there's no such thing as happily-ever-after."

There was a baby cook at my hotel in the paralyzingly beautiful Irish countryside. His face wasn't even fully formed, I didn't feel right about going out with him, but what the hell. I didn't want to kiss him, but what the hell.

The real mistake was sleeping with him. I felt the chasm of the decades between us. He was so far away I felt I was sleeping with another species. It was like bestiality. It was really funny.

I am definitely not a man.

Dear Problem Lady:

How much do you tell a friend who is completely deluded?

Denise is having an affair with a married man. She thinks he's not married. She thinks it's a marriage "in name only." Denise actually used those very words, which tells you how far gone she is. She thinks this guy is totally faithful to her.

She also thinks the wife lives in Brazil. The wife doesn't live in Brazil, the wife is in New York at least half the year. This is the guy's second wife, he also still sleeps with his first wife.

Plus he has a few bimbos whom he keeps around just for laughs. In other words, he's a psychopath.

I found all this out from my friend Steve, who is seeing the first wife's sister.

Meanwhile Denise, poor idiot, is going around with this goofy smile on her face telling everyone she's "never felt this way before" and that "he really loves me for who I am." She is such a sap.

Should I tell her the truth? I think she wouldn't believe me and also hate me. Plus Steve told me all this stuff in confidence and swore me to secrecy. I'm torn.

Howard

Dear Howard:

If this were a legal matter, you'd be laughed right out of the judge's chambers.

The first wife's sister? Come on. This is a woman with as much regard for truth as Bush's press secretary. She could have made the whole thing up.

Although she probably didn't. One thing I've learned in my vast years of experience is that whenever you hear even the vaguest glimmer of a rumor of infidelity, it's usually true, and then some. We are a sneaky, dishonorable species.

So here's the real reason why you shouldn't tell Denise: She already knows.

Women who get involved with married men always construct the most complicated states of denial: His wife is frigid, his wife is insane, his wife is a Republican, I'm not really doing this, etc. But deep in their heart of hearts they know they're having an affair with a man who can't be trusted, with a man who likes the drama of infidelity too much to quit.

(This is irrelevant, but the only time I've ever heard of these situations working is when both people are married and they both immediately leave their spouses. Then they usually stay together for fifty fun-filled years.)

Denise secretly knows all this. That's what's behind her goofy smile.

Problem Lady

Dear Problem Lady:

There is this guy who keeps asking me out and everyone's driving me nuts about him, especially my mother.

"Go out with him, what could it hurt?" she'll say twelve times in a phone call. "He's a nice fellow with a good job, Miss Picky. Or is Robert Redford beating down your door?"

"Ma, Robert Redford is an old guy now," I tell her.

"All the more reason you should date Mitchell."

And I can't believe it, but my friends are on her side. "No one's talking about love, just get out of the goddamned house for an evening," says my friend Rita.

"I don't think that dating should be a recreational activity," I tell Rita. "If I want a night out I can always go bowling." And then my mother calls and starts in again. "So you don't like him, okay, maybe he has a friend," she says.

"Ma! Enough!" I scream.

Don't you think that when you meet the right person you just know? *Mitchell is very nice and easy to talk to, but I feel no sparks, I feel no chemistry, and I don't see the point of going out with someone unless you're just dying to rip his clothes off.*

Mary

Dear Mary:

I think that when you meet the right person, one *of you just* knows.

It might not be you. You might be one of those girls with bad instincts. One of those girls who, when she walks into a roomful of men, immediately gravitates toward the alcoholic ex-junkie who can never return a phone call. There are a lot of us out there who should be put in a home for women who make inane choices.

But even if you're relatively healthy you should still pay attention to a man who's making such an enormous push. He may know something you don't know, he may feel something you don't feel yet because your mother and friends are making you so recalcitrant and cranky.

What the hell, give it five dates.

Problem Lady

Dear Problem Lady:

My friends have kind of hinted around that they don't like my girlfriend.

Five of them took me out to dinner the other day and demanded that I immediately stop seeing her.

Okay, maybe "hint" is the wrong word.

Where do they get off?

Melanie is a great girl! She's pretty and laughs a lot and cooks great dinners and she really likes me, I can tell.

But my friends assure me that she will break my heart. That she's a phony and is just killing time with me. They say that I should get out now before she does any real damage.

I say that friends who are not concerned with a pal's happiness, who are just jealous because a pal finally has something else to do on Saturday nights besides eat pizza with them, are not friends at all. I'm thinking of dropping them like the hot potatoes they are.

Steve

Dear Steve:

Listen to your friends! Break up with this girl immediately! Even if you can't bear it, do it!

Everyone in the world, after seeing someone for a couple of months, should convene a tribunal of friends to decide absolutely on the fate of their love affair.

Nine out of ten people have notoriously bad instincts. Nine out of ten times they will choose mates for themselves who are wrong and bad and will cost thousands of dollars in shrink bills.

Most friends will just sit quietly and talk behind your back, figuring you'll react just the way you're reacting.

These friends of yours are brave souls. Clasp them to your bosom. Buy them dinner.

Problem Lady

Dear Problem Lady:

I am involved in a long-distance relationship. He lives in Boston, I live in New York. I fly up there one weekend a month, he flies down to New York whenever he feels like it.

No. That's not fair. He usually flies down for a few days every month, too, it's just that I'm so annoyed with him. Here's why:

I could move up there. I've been offered a job, a good job. Not that I'm crazy about Boston, everybody's very snooty and every time you have to drive around the corner to get milk you get hopelessly lost and end up in Marblehead or somewhere and people have to send out search parties, and then the search parties get lost, and anyway there aren't even any good clothing stores or nightclubs.

But I love him, and if we could live together I could get used to ending up in Marblehead incessantly and getting all my outfits from catalogs.

Guess what? (I bet you already have.) He doesn't want me to move. It's so sickening I actually puked a few times last night.

He doesn't say, "I don't want you up here, Clarice." No. He says his place is too small. We'll move, I say. It's not a good time, he says, the real estate market is so bad, he would take a bath if he sold his place. But, I point out, if the market's bad, it's bad for everyone, not just you, you moron, and since everybody's taking a bath, you could get a place real cheap and that would cancel out the bath you think you'll take.

"You just don't understand anything," he says.

I understand everything. "How about if I got my own apartment near you?" I ask.

"That would be interesting," he says.

"But do you want me to?" I ask.

"It might be kinda nice."

"Look, could you just say 'I want you to' or 'I don't want you to?' "

"I'll call you later, the doorbell's ringing."

"Wait!"

But he's already hung up the phone. The doorbell has rung really opportunely in the past few weeks.

So look, this man loves me, I know he does. So what is he doing? I can't believe it. I thought he'd be so thrilled. He hates me.

Clarice

Dear Clarice:

He doesn't hate you. But he might hate you if you moved to Boston.

In every relationship, some distance is required if one or both of the partners are not to feel claustrophobic and threatened. Some couples need separate apartments, some only rooms of their own, some are content with separate kitchens, and some are perfectly happy with a studio apartment as long as whoever needs to can lock herself in the bathroom.

And some people really need a lot of space. I know an Englishman who can only have girlfriends who live in America. If they're on the same continent he starts feeling crowded. From the evidence, your dude needs a couple of states.

Don't move up there until you get to the bottom of the problem, or unless the job is good enough that you'd be happy to be up there even if you break up with him.

Don't talk on the phone, talk in person. Watch him closely. If he seems calm, sensible, and just a tad reluctant, he's just having a normal person's fear of change. But if you notice his eyes rolling back in his head, if he breaks out in shivering sweats and keeps running to the bathroom, he's panicking, and there's nothing you can do except ask him to go to a shrink and then wait five years.

Problem Lady

L.A.

Welcome to the Earth Moving

The other night I woke up in the middle of the night (7:45 a.m.) and thought, Thank God I am in New York where I belong. Then the bed started gently shaking. The dogs started barking. Car alarms started shrieking. It felt as though I were on the back of a flatbed truck going over a dirt road. Then the bed jumped about a foot in the air. Something in another room crashed and shattered.

Where the hell am I? I thought, desperate with sleepiness. I picked up the phone. No dial tone. I put it down. It rang. I picked it up.

"Welcome to L.A.," someone crooned.

"Thank you very much," I said and put the phone down. It rang. I picked it up.

"Welcome to L.A.," somebody else sang.

"What the hell is this?" I asked. "Don't you people ever sleep?"

"Come on, get excited," said the voice I was beginning to recognize as my friend Paula's, "it's your first earthquake."

EARTHQUAKE!

It occurred to me that I was in Los Angeles.

This happens to me every morning. I wake up, think Thank God I'm back in New York City, and I never am. I'm out here. I had to leave New York, I couldn't stand it anymore. Everyone had been driven insane by the eighties. Now I'm here, where everyone's always been insane.

I miss New York the way a kid misses its mother. I feel displaced and homeless. I feel like I'm at some other kid's summer camp. I want to get home before dark. I feel guilty writing this, how dare I leave . . .

On this earthquake morning I turned on the TV. They were having a riotous time on every network. The earthquake measured six-point-something on the Richter scale. "Do not, we repeat, do not use the phone unless it's an emergency," the anchors were saying. Two seconds later they told us to "Call in if you have any earthquake stories to report." People did.

"I was watching the pool when it happened and the water sloshed right over the side."

"I was just sitting at my dining room table and the dishes in the cabinet started rattling. They didn't break, though."

"I slept right through the whole damned thing."

This went on for hours. People missed their soap operas while cretins told the most tedious stories anyone has ever told in the history of the universe.

They would never stand still for this shit in New York, I thought. The phone rang.

"Are you watching this shit on TV?" my son in New York asked.

People here are relentlessly nice to each other. The ones in the "industry" will cut your throat as soon as look at you, but they act just darling to your face. Once it took me twenty minutes to get my frozen yogurt (I know, and I'm sorry, but it's happening to me) and my enormous New York impulse was to yell, "Yo! What the *fuck* are you doing back there? Jerking off?" Which I would have done ten minutes sooner at Melanie's on Sixth Avenue if they ever dared to take so long which they wouldn't. But out here you just don't. Teenagers with implausibly tiny brains work in all the shops out here and they mean no harm, they're simply clueless. So when someone pisses me off I just turn away and very quietly mutter, "Fuck you you stupid cunt you fucking cocksucker I hate you." And I feel much better. I think everyone here is secretly doing this.

The New York I miss is not the New York I left. I ran away from a city ravaged by real estate scams and people in Jackets. Those status jackets from the eighties that you wore to make sure everyone knew you were hip and rich. Before those jackets marched onto the scene I used to walk down the street and hear someone practicing the cello, someone singing an aria, I'd see some lunatic trying out his comic monologue on his stoop. Those deadly groovy jackets destroyed all the goofy creativity that made me move to New York in the first place. Everyone began madly scrambling to make a lot of money so they could buy jackets that enabled them to get into exclusive restaurants. Now people are running around with no jobs and mortgages they can't pay and jackets they can't eat. Now the streets are silent except for drug casualties.

But out here I sometimes want to die when I see the hairdos, and the fingernails, and the glistening guys in their beards and black Porsches. I'm living in a beer commercial.

A beer commercial where you're not allowed to fail. You tell each other how great you're doing or else you're shunned. When these people smell failure, they stampede in the other direction, trampling parking valets to death. So you just say how great everything is.

I don't know how long I'll be here. A few more months. But it's really nice. I'm doing really well. Everything is great. Oh my God.

On earthquake morning the door to my house was wedged shut. I couldn't get out. Oh my God.

Strung Out in the Big Orange

I should be happy in Los Angeles. No demented homeless men fly at me from stoops and try to take my dog. I don't have to sidestep eyebrow-wielding trendies setting up picnic lunches in front of Barneys' windows. I no longer have psychotic episodes from being stuck in a cab on Sixth Avenue for forty-five minutes teetering over a hole full of exposed and rotted pipes while the driver confesses his addiction to laxatives.

Out here I have a car, and I don't know if anyone in Manhattan knows this, but a car is just a moving, giant handbag! You never have actually to carry groceries, or dry cleaning, or anything! You can have five pairs of shoes with you at all times!

And I'm living in this Brady Bunch house with a yard. In the yard are a lemon tree, an orange tree, a tangerine tree, a lime tree. I want an orange, I pick it, I eat it.

But something in Los Angeles is very, very wrong. It's not the face-lifts, or the infestation of Miatas, or the white cowboy boots, or even the pizzas with pineapple and goat cheese. I have just figured out what it is.

Unlike the rest of America, nobody here is on drugs.

Your typical American comes home every day miserable, restless, wired, and strange from a hideous day of taking all kinds of shit at the office. She very badly needs something to blot out the pain of her pointless and repetitive existence, her endless disappointments and small but continual frustrations. She needs something to make her mind go numb and blank and vague and stupid. So she switches on the TV.

Immediately her clenched jaw relaxes and she begins, just slightly, to drool. Her eyes glaze and her pupils reduce to a pinpoint as "Night Court" or "MacGyver" permeates her bloodstream, destroying brain cells and inducing catatonic euphoria. If she needs a really big fix, she'll rent a video, or even go out and see *Terminator 2*.

Los Angeles people are incapable of passively mainlining TV and movies. Here you have to read who produced or directed every episode, who wrote it, who had guest shots and whether you know them personally and if they like you. You have to figure out who everybody's agent is and whether yours is better. You not only know but deeply care about the difference between such job titles as Producer, Supervising Producer, and Executive Story Editor. You can compute by a person's title what kind of car she drives and where on the studio lot she's allowed to park. You know by heart every show's time slot and where it stacks up in the ratings, who's been fired recently and how to avoid them.

So while the rest of the country is lying stupid in a media-induced coma, people in L.A. are in constant withdrawal. This makes them cranky. They chew their nails and fret. They pour into twelve-step meetings of every description. They run on treadmills and kill themselves on Stairmasters, trying to tire themselves out, trying to avoid incessant consciousness. While the rest of the country sleeps peacefully, they have insomnia. They can't even indulge in the consolation prize of the late seventies and early eighties—massive amounts of cocaine.

Nor can they indulge in this nation's other favorite pastime. Everyone's a critic, except in L.A.

Although everyone is seething with opinions, they smile and keep their mouths shut and live in utter denial. If you whine and complain they call you difficult and send you back to New York where homeless men leap at you.

No one dares say, "Streisand's last movie? What a stupid idea! Has she lost her marbles? I could never understand her appeal anyway." Because the person at the next table just might be Barbra's development person who could possibly give you a job one day. And you want that job. It could pay you one skillion dollars, which is hard to pass up. And if you're already making one skillion dollars, you're terrified to lose it, because you're making payments on a $4 million house and three $50,000 cars, not to mention your Lakers tickets. And success in L.A. is completely arbitrary. One day you're the brilliant genius of life, the next day people act like there's a bad smell when you approach. Lots of expensive, late-model cars are offered in the *L.A. Times* every day by people who have suddenly begun to smell bad.

The stakes are just too high for human dignity.

So people only let loose alone, in the dark, where no one knows them. I went to *T2* at the Cinerama Dome on Sunset Boulevard last week. The place was packed with people in foul tempers screaming. "Bad looping!" someone yelled. "Where's the second act, you moron?!" someone else shrieked.

I joined right in.

Jay and Me

The day dawned bright and clear, as it always does. The birds were singing, as they always do. The dogs jumped on my head and tried to lick my nostrils, as they always do. And I always roll toward them and they play the game "let's bite whatever we see."

But not this morning. This morning my eyes were nailed shut. This morning my stomach felt like the Alien was living there. This morning was the day of my "Tonight Show" appearance.

I have been on television before, and every time I look at the tape later and want to die. I acquire sudden, extra chins. My eyes become beady, my body a sack of flour, I smile constantly and inanely. I speak gibberish. You know, just like you're afraid you'll be when you're on TV.

So now "The Tonight Show." Coming through that curtain. Walking across the set. Saying hello to everyone, sitting down, chatting. I lay there with my eyes shut, terrified.

Coming through that curtain. How does anybody do that? How is anybody not completely paralyzed with self-consciousness? How does anybody not break into shrill hysterics and then fall on the floor and have an epileptic seizure? What if the curtain snags on your tooth? What if your dress just falls right off?

"Good morning! You're doomed!" sang my son.

"Get the fuck out of here," I trilled.

"Only seven hours to get ready," he taunted.

Sometimes being in the shower can calm you down. Today my brain just kept chanting, "It's today! Today! Today!"

My friend Merrill had just been on the show. Neither of us was able to eat. Merrill called it "the talk show diet."

"Oh, come on, why be nervous?" I asked. "What is it, ten million people watching you if you happen to throw up all over Jay?"

After her show, Merrill called. "It was fine," she said. "I wasn't in my body even for a second, but it was fine."

"It's only eight minutes out of your life," my shrink told me.

"Fuck you, you do it," I told him.

I kept looking for my world-weary, countercultural cynicism. I kept waiting for a voice to bubble up from my unconscious and say, "It's just a stupid, mainstream TV show, you're way too cool to care about something so trivial."

I got dressed eight times. I blow-dried my hair until it whimpered. Every friend I ever had called to say "Don't worry, you'll be fine." I put all my clothes on hangers, three pairs of shoes in a bag. The doorbell rang. It was the guy with the car.

"Get the hell out of the bathroom," I yelled to my son. He emerged from the bathroom ten minutes later looking fabulous.

"Wait a minute!" I shrieked as the car was about to pull out of the driveway. The driver screeched to a halt. I ran into the house and got my black tights, thus narrowly avoiding the monumental catastrophe of appearing in front of ten million people with a skirt slit up to my waist and bare legs.

When we got to NBC I noticed a Yugo parked in Jay Leno's space. I decided I was hallucinating.

Inside I found all the people from "The Tonight Show" who had been calling me all week saying "Don't worry! You'll be fine!" I tried to act like a regular person, joking around and such. I spoke in tongues.

In my dressing room was a giant basket of fruit and cakes, a card from Jay saying "Yes, I read it!" (meaning my book), and many snacks. I bound up my breasts so that my jacket buttons wouldn't pop. A guy who had interviewed me on the phone came in with a list of the questions Jay would ask me. Then he told me what my answers would be, the same answers I had given him on the phone. I had no idea what he was talking about.

My son came in and I grabbed his jacket. "Give me a joke, any joke, I need a joke," I pleaded.

On the way to makeup I saw Christian Laettner, the giant basketball guy. The other guests were the band They Might Be Giants.

"They *might* be giants, but he *is* a giant," I thought. A joke!

"Listen to this," I told my son. "They *might* be giants, but he definitely is!"

"Who?" he wondered.

Jay Leno came to say hello. His face was all orange from makeup, his eyes cornflower blue. "Don't worry, you'll be fine," he said. "Won't you?" He looked a little nervous.

"Sure I will," I told him.

Standing there, waiting to go on, I thought of certain people who would be livid with rage that I got to go on "The Tonight Show" and they didn't. I'm not proud of this feeling, but it got me through the curtain.

Don't worry, I was fine. And now I'm insufferable.

Schizo

Oh, hello.

I'm still in Los Angeles. And something incredible is happening to me. Suddenly I've become a vegetarian. Okay not quite a vegetarian but somehow, *against my will*, I find I can't eat beef anymore. Or lamb or pork. Obviously I don't eat veal, nobody is ever allowed to eat veal again.

Which reminds me, although I am an animal-rights person, I feel that many of us should get real and lighten up. For example, I have this book in front of me, Save the Animals! 101 Easy Things You Can Do, *and there is a foreword by Linda McCartney, the most irritating woman on the planet. Here's what Linda writes:*

> We stopped eating meat the day we happened to look out our window during Sunday Lunch and saw our young lambs playing happily, as kittens do, in the fields. Eating bits of them suddenly made no sense.

Naturally I have not been able to read past that part, I just collapse into fits of ecstasy over the magnificent stupidity.

So I've always liked a nice cheeseburger and never in my wildest of dreams have ever considered wearing a long, flowing flowered skirt. But guess what? Yes, something in the smog out here has turned beef totally revolting to me and three perfectly hideous flowered skirts hang in my closet, and I like them fine. I wear them and everything.

So far I haven't purchased any white cowboy boots but I feel it's only a matter of time.

No sushi though. Thank God I still have my New York paranoia and remember hearing about *parasites in raw fish that will rot anyone's brain.*

In this Save the Animals *book it also tells us to "Eat sea vegetables instead of sea animals."*

And they mean it. I want to slap them. We are animals! We are omnivores! Right at the base of our reptilian brains is an encoded message which says, "Smash another animal over the head and devour it, quick, you idiot!"

Not that I don't understand the point. There is nothing wrong with being a vegetarian. I seem to be one. And the way every single farm animal is treated is appalling, heinous, criminal. I think we should only be allowed to eat an animal if we have stomach enough to kill it in the wild. But any social movement that shrieks at you and calls you a murderer if you eat shrimp or wear leather shoes is bound for failure.

And then, just to confuse matters further, I went to London. On Virgin, the only airline company that's trying to be "green." On the flight over, my schizoid New York–L.A. self laughed at their complimentary aromatherapy kit, but after three days in London I believed passionately in this little kit which allegedly cures jet lag. Yes, I became hopelessly in thrall to yet another city. I found myself becoming English.

L.A.

In England they laugh uproariously at *Iron John*. It's the funniest thing they've ever heard of in their entire lives. Not that any of them have ever read the book, they just are overpowered by gales of giggles at the very idea. And just try telling them about cars with air bags. They slap their thighs and fall over and bang their heads chortling. Shrinks, even, make them snicker. But they are mad, insane, over aroma-therapy. They all go and pay tons of money to people who give them scented oils to cure their foul tempers, which everyone knows is caused by every day consisting entirely of no sun whatsoever.

Out of the blue, I found myself laughing at air bags and wanting, oh, maybe a kipper for breakfast. My hair in L.A. had become, well, you know how nobody out here has ever gotten over Farrah Fawcett's famous do? I had been fighting a losing battle with my hair, which suddenly had a mind of its own and wanted to be long and flowing, but after three days in London I went and got some kind of neo-seventies haircut. They've gone all seventies in London. I felt myself wishing for a smelly sheepskin coat from Afghanistan.

But then I thought, "Oh, sorry, Linda, I forgot about the frolicking lambs." Do you know that some animal-rights types make their dogs eat vegetarian dog food? And others put out magazines which on every page show full-color corpses of slaughtered animals. So you can't possibly buy these magazines.

And I want to. I want to be an activist. I want to make sure no more dolphins are being caught in nets, no more gorillas or elephants are sadistically slaughtered. I want to work tirelessly to save endangered species.

But not if I have to hang out with self-righteous prigs. How about priorities? We could concentrate on boycotting Procter and Gamble and all animal-testing cosmetics companies. We could blow the whistle on universities and government agencies who give scientists tons of money to do pointless and depraved animal "research." We could force all those evil

167

subhuman puppy-mill owners to live in those tiny feces-encrusted cages where they imprison dogs. And what the hell, we could spray paint a couple of fur coats.

Let meat-eaters join in. There will be a lot more of us.

In London I kept waking up thinking, "I'm in New York! No, no, I'm in L.A.! Wait, where's the sun? Where the hell am I?" Each city has its own collective unconscious. So does each species. It's too confusing to be human. I can't concentrate.

Dances with Oscar

We were bored, bored, bored! We sat around eating fried chicken, we lay around drinking wine and beer and even champagne, trying to perk up this year's Oscar party, but the specter of Kevin Costner hung heavily, dampening our spirits and dulling our senses.

Oh, Kevin, why? Why can't you just be the character in *Bull Durham?* Why do we ever have to hear you say your own words? The moment you thanked Michael Ovitz was the moment that 100 million American women fell out of love with you. The moment you referred to your own "boyish enthusiasm" was the moment 100 million women fell into a severe depression because the fantasies they'd been nurturing for years were shattered into bits! Oh, why, Kevin, why?

(And, just wondering, do the Indians get any money?)

We didn't know what a tough night for womanhood it would be when we turned on the TV. We didn't know that Robert De Niro would appear with his hair in a flip like Marilyn Quayle, we didn't know we would have to come to terms with a whole new Jeff Bridges in a Nehru collar. We didn't know that only Daniel Day-Lewis would survive our fantasies intact. But we did know that we'd all vote for *Dances with Wolves* in the Oscar pool.

"At the Academy I voted for what I wanted, now I'm voting for what I think will win," said Alan, our resident Academy member.

"I have two words," said Sonny the actor. "Wolf sweep."

And we're all so poor right now that we voted utterly cynically, not wildly predicting our own faves, because we *needed to win* that dollar a person.

So we all voted for Whoopi, who won and who acted predictably irritating.

"I wanted this," Whoopi said, "you don't know . . ."

"We know, Whoopi, we know!" we screamed back at her.

(Speaking of which, did anyone else think that her interview with Barbara Walters was prurient, obscene, and dishonest? That intimate, personal baring of the soul about teenage pregnancy and junkiehood, wasn't it indecent exposure? Didn't the spectacle of what people will do for attention and ratings make your palms itch?)

"If *Wolves* wins for sound I predict a sweep," said Henry the piano player.

"I predict a *Home Alone* sweep," said Brodie the college student.

"Geena Davis is wearing a curtain, no a tablecloth!" said Joanne the costumer. "Kim Basinger's wearing the same dress as last year without the sleeve." Kim Basinger is so weird. We all hear that she and Alec have tremendous fights and then tremendous sex.

Madonna's hands were shaking. What can it mean?

"See what else is on," said Henry.

"There's that two-hour 'Gilligan's Island' thing," said Sonny.

"Billy Crystal has a maroon scarf matching his maroon jacket," said Joanne.

"Look, it's the *Home Alone* dancers!" said Brodie.

Bob Hope came on and we cringed at the hair plugs in his scalp.

"No one's getting up, he's not getting a standing ovation," said Sonny. But Bob just stood there and eked it out of the audience.

"Maybe he'll die onstage," said Joe the writer. "Just a thought."

We almost came to blows over Reba McEntire's dress—the shoulder-pad versus the no-shoulder-pad contingent. We all loved Susan Sarandon, we always love Susan Sarandon. And of course Jodie "hello, here are my tits" Foster looked fab. We loved how Candy Bergen said that it took her thirty years to recover from *Snow White*. And of course Sally Field delighted us by saying that *Gone With the Wind* was all about her and therefore living up to her "You like me!" reputation.

But did they have to take the camera into Myrna Loy's apartment, throwing us all into the deepest despair?

"Bon Jovi. Is he a singer or is he a fragrance?" asked Alan. "Cher's boyfriend is making some really good guitar faces."

We hated Glenn Close and decided she looks like a reptile.

We screamed in pain when *Ghost* won for best screenplay.

"The draft I read, Whoopi dies," said Sonny.

Sophia Loren looked very sixties. "They say she fucked everyone," someone said.

"And who she didn't fuck she wanted to," someone else said.

"She's horny right now," Henry said.

So *Dances* won and we all yawned.

"A vote for *Dances with Wolves* is a vote for America," said Sonny.

"It's a fix!" Alan screamed. "Scorsese's never won! He lost to *Robert Redford* last time."

"Maybe Kevin Costner cheats on his wife," said someone. "I know someone who says she did it with him."

We saw that the producer had a big herpeslike sore on his lip and turned off the TV.

"Reality is such a drag after the awards," said Joanne. "Tomorrow I'm going to put on an evening gown to go to the supermarket."

La La Land Under Siege

On the worst day of the L.A. riots, when thousands of fires raged and most of Los Angeles resembled war-raddled Beirut, a bunch of women gathered for a baby shower given by one of our most famous movie stars at her most fabulous home. Everyone was in peach, mint, or white. Everyone wore the palest ivory stockings. They sat under umbrellas. Little tea sandwiches and scones were deferentially served by Mexican women. There was a scary second when a woman wandered too far into the garden and was almost shredded by an attack Rottweiler, but a uniformed security guard intervened and everybody laughed.

Then the housekeeper appeared. "Ma'am," she said, "the city is burning. People are getting killed. There's gonna be a curfew."

"My God," said a producer's wife. "I've gotta go. My nanny will be frantic."

"But why is this happening to us?" asked an astrologer.

Unlike New York, Los Angeles is startlingly segregated. South Central Los Angeles, where the riots and looting started, takes up about one-quarter of the city. Nobody who doesn't live there would ever be caught dead going there. Nobody who does live there ever leaves except to go wait on rich people. Before Wednesday, affluent Los Angeles denied the actual existence of South Central Los Angeles. The gulf between the Haves and Have-nots is terrifying: The Haves enjoy the hugely inflated salaries of the entertainment industry; the Have-nots subsist on minimum wage or welfare.

On Thursday, two women in Armani rompers did leg-lifts with a sixty-dollar-an-hour trainer in Beverly Hills.

"Let's put on wigs and go loot Neiman Marcus. We'll grab some Barry Keiselstein-Cord belts."

"Yeah! And a dozen or two Judith Leiber bags."

"Did you see when a looter showed up at Sears in a yellow cab?" asked the trainer.

Over in Gelson's, a posh supermarket in posh Studio City, everyone was running amok. People were driving up in their Saabs and Jaguars, leaving their cars everywhere, hysterically grabbing twenty-dollar bottles of extra-virgin olive oil off the shelves.

"What do you mean, Beverly Hills is under curfew?" one shopper yelled to another. "I'm going to a very important dinner there tonight!"

During the curfew, I talked to my friends on the phone.

"I like it," said Kathryn, an actress. "I can be a slug and watch TV. It's against the law to go out."

"Those actors who are making speeches are getting on my nerves," said Marco, a writer. "It's like, 'We're superheroes because we're actors, if you just listen to us we can stop all this.' Those actors don't know shit about what's going on."

We all watched the looting on television. We saw women carrying tables, men loaded down with dozens of pairs of trousers. Lots of color TVs being hefted into trunks of cars.

"Maybe I should go down there," said Pat, a director. "I need some luggage and new sheets."

"I feel like I'm being punished," said Lana, a secretary. "I'm not allowed out. The movie theaters are closed, the malls are closed. Look, there are looters in Volvos! There's one in a BMW! A Volkswagen Cabriolet! They're getting stereos and computers, I've got nothing!"

"They've raided Frederick's of Hollywood!" said Kathryn. "Somebody's got an armload of crotchless panties!"

During the curfew, we watched the looting and fires spread to middle-class neighborhoods, to rich neighborhoods. That's when people got scared.

"Oh my God, Sammy's camera repair!" said a screenwriter. "They've got my Nikon there! Shit!"

"What if the tailor shop that's redoing my dress for the wedding burns down?" asked an actress.

During the curfew, I discovered ugly things about people I thought I knew.

"I can see the fires from here," said a painter. "And earlier today, there were lots of undesirables driving around."

"What do you mean, undesirables?"

"Well, people who look weird. Fringe people. People in old beat-up cars. And then four black guys in a white BMW, you know, like they drive, went to *my* supermarket and yelled, 'We're in your neighborhood now!' "

"It's black people's own fault they're in the trouble they're in. Look how well the Koreans do," said an animator.

But then, some people were contrite.

"I feel like I should go up to black people and apologize," said Paula, a musician. "This has been coming for so long. Our government is so unresponsive. The Rodney King ruling just lit the match. This country isn't working."

"We should just find Reagan and give him to the rioters," said Harriet, a journalist. "Isn't it all his fault? His whole message to poor people was 'Fuck you, we're all getting as rich as we can, and some money might trickle down if you're lucky. If not, tough.' "

During the curfew, we had nothing to do but watch TV and see our city burn. And think. It wasn't pleasant.

Dear Problem Lady:

I have a friend, let's call her Judy, who just got famous. She has her own TV news show. I'm really proud of her. Plus whenever I'm feeling insecure I get to drop Judy's name and people are impressed. Just knowing her gets me a good table in restaurants.

So while Judy's fame has done wonders for me, she seems to be falling apart. She's lost her personality entirely.

At least half the people she knows won't talk to her anymore. I asked her why.

"They're jealous of me," she says, "they won't rest until I fail."

"Get the fuck out of here with your melodrama," I say. "Friends are allowed to get jealous, they'll get over it if you take that damned tiara off your head."

"Don't you talk to me that way," she said.

Judy was never the kind of woman who said "Don't talk to me that way." Judy was more the kind of woman who said "Oh God, have I upset you? I'm sorry." She had low self-esteem, which I prefer in a friend.

Not only is she not speaking to people, she's not going anywhere. Judy used to be a girl who would go to a party and literally put a lampshade on her head. She would dance and carry on and flirt with unsuitable men. Now she stays home and has food ordered in. She used to talk on the phone for hours, now she gets bored after ten minutes.

Once I got her to go out for dinner. She had a full-blown anxiety attack and had to go home. She was afraid someone had poisoned her cats.

Meanwhile, on TV, she's just as happy and sweet and bubbly as ever.

I'd hate to give up on her because I love her, and I'd lose all those name-dropping opportunities. But should I?

J.R.V.

Dear J.R.V.:

Your friend has two major problems. The first one is being on TV.

A human being who is regularly on TV enters some kind of hyperreality the moment the camera is on her. Actual reality seems kind of flat and flavorless, actual reality is no longer "real." A TV person doesn't feel like she's living unless she's on TV, regular life has lost its point.

When Judy is with you, she's just marking time until she's on TV again.

The second problem is that when your normal low-self-esteem person suddenly gets a lot of power, it has a traumatic effect on the psyche. I once knew a sweet, rather unassuming newspaper reporter who suddenly became editor in chief. He turned into a paranoiac, tyrannical monster. He projected all kinds of evil feelings onto everyone he came near. He was sure there were incessant plots against him and treated everyone as his enemy. He became the most hated man in lower Manhattan.

I don't know why this happens to people. Guilt at succeeding when they don't think they deserve it? Repressed anger suddenly unrepressed and running amok?

There's nothing to do about Judy except wait for her to get over herself. If she becomes really famous, that may never happen.

Problem Lady

Dear Problem Lady:

How can I regain my youth?

I'm not talking about looks. I think the most middle-aged thing you can do is worry about wrinkles and sags and whether you look your goddamned age or not. I mean I go to parties where the chief topic is face-lifts-or-not and it's boring, boring.

I'm talking about attitude. I am now a small-minded, frightened person. I worry about the future. I worry about my bank account. I worry about taxes and mortgages and my health and am plagued by my own morbid attention to the stultifying details of my mundane little life. My mind doesn't sweep, or soar, or do anything more interesting than fret at three a.m.

I can't blame my job, or my lover, or my children. I'm living in the small bare prison cell of middle age.

I went to Woodstock, for chrissakes! I slept in a field with cows! I peed in bushes cavalierly! I tried heroin! I went to Who concerts and pushed through the crowds to the front! I hitchhiked across this goddamned country! Twice! I was stranded in Indiana both times and I didn't care! I've had crabs!

Now sometimes I go to the movies. If I'm sure there won't be a big line. I am pathetic.

But every once in a while, usually when I'm driving along an unfamiliar road and a good song comes on the radio, I become drenched with the same feelings I had twenty years ago. I remember who I used to be. And my heart almost bursts and I believe that anything in the whole world is possible and I roll down all the windows of my car, turn the radio up, and sing at the top of my lungs.

I really am pathetic.

So is there any way to regain those feelings on a regular basis? Feelings of freedom, feelings that anything could happen? Or does my aging condemn me to becoming more narrow, more doddering, and more trivial with every passing day?

Doris

Dear Doris:

Young people just want to have fun, old people just want to be safe. Young people don't believe in death. Old people see death around every corner.

Young people feel safe with a knapsack, ten bucks, and a roast beef sandwich. Old people crave their own beds and multiple insurance policies. As we get old, our need for security increases exponentially. We become burdened down by the weight of our props.

If you want to feel young again, you need less weight. You have to give up some of your coziness and start living closer to the edge. Quit your job if you hate it, sell your house if you're a mortgage slave, stop stockpiling money and possessions. Most of all (this is scary) you have to stop being afraid.

If you do, possibilities will drop on you from every tree.

Here's an idea: Why not play some music from your youth, the music that brings up the feelings? And then, when those great feelings kick in, do something impulsive and irrevocable.

You'll have a really good time. If you don't die.

Problem Lady